THE COLORS OF MY HEART

EMBRACING MY BLACKNESS THROUGH HISTORY, FAMILY, FEAR, AND FAITH

MARGARET DELARESE LARKINS-PETTIGREW, MD

ISBN-13: 978-1-7347763-0-0

Cover design by: Ángel López
Printed in the United States of America.

DEDICATION

Dedicated to Wilbur Lee Larkins & Beatrice Martha Minnis Larkins who chose to call me daughter! Chenits who has become the air that I breathe! Granny who gifted me with her only son! Carlos Rondell, Chenits Reese, and Gaetan Lorenz who are my living heroes! Corbin Cassidy, Chase Janella, and Carson Rider who make "the colors of my heart" feel like a rainbow each and every day!

CONTENTS

PROLOGUE

Sometimes, I feel discriminated against, but it does not make me angry. It merely astonishes me. How can any deny themselves the pleasure of my company? It's beyond me.
~ ZORA NEALE HURSTON

Outside, the sun shines. Inside, there's only darkness. The blackness is hard to describe, as it's more than symptoms. It's a nothing that becomes everything there is. And what one sees is only a fraction of the trauma inflicted.
~ JUSTIN ORDONEZ

She has been pushing for two hours. Finally, the baby is crowning. The room is full of close relatives and friends. Three generations are present – great-grandma and two anxious grandmothers-to-be are excellent coaches. "Push, push...1-2-3-4-5-6-7-8-9-10," they recite in unison as this first-time mom holds her breath. Demonstrating great perseverance, dedication, and focus, she resembles a beautiful African queen ready to meet her offspring. With Olympian strength, she presses her chin against her chest, leans back her broad hips, and holds her legs apart to open a path through her pelvis and vagina for the emerging child. All around her are prayers and chants, ritual blessings to welcome this new life. He crowns. I guide his head through the opening of her vagina, watching as his shoulders, back, and finally his little hands and feet emerge from the warm and nourishing womb. A shallow breath erupted into a screaming complaint against the cold world. Mom and Dad embrace their gift and welcome him with tears and kisses. At five minutes, the pediatrician declares an Apgar score of 9 out of 10; at ten minutes, it's still 9, close to perfect in appearance, pulse rate, grimace, activity, and respiration.

The family gathers around this tiny creature. In this moment of supreme love and joy, they say: "I hope he will be light like your mom. I don't want him to be dark like Uncle Joe." Great-grandma touches his ear. "You can tell by the back of his ears. Oh, yeah! His is going to be a light one," she exults. I wonder whether this was how my own life began. What were my parents thinking as the welcomed me into this world? Did they worry about the shade of my skin and how it would affect my life's journey?

Color – skin color – hue, tint, shade – is an indelible feature of every person's first impression. It can trigger instant solidarity – *This person looks like me!* – or instant hostility – *That's one of those people!* Color, like its cognate features of race, ethnicity, religion, and nationality, can foster a sense of belonging or doom an individual to a second-class life of exclusion.

Color cannot be denied. The well-meaning or virtue-signaling person who protests, "I don't see color!" is advancing the same erasure of the other as the bigot who proclaims, "Niggers don't have souls!" Inclusion means including people of color *as people of color*, just as *white people* are included as white people, respecting their full identity rather than reducing them to some common denominator. People who grasp this concept that color matters will start to see the whole person of color. With this awakening, individuals can begin to grasp the reality of people of color and enjoy a rich and full experience with people they get to know. As a practicing obstetrician/gynecologist, I have seen how color can influence intellectual, educational, and emotional growth. Seeing color reveals the real self beyond the guarded behaviors, the fear, and the lack of trust that many embody. Seeing color can move white people to acknowledge the devastating history of black folks with passion and humility, inspiring advocacy for social justice for those who have been disenfranchised.

I have seen both the beauty and the perils of color in my life as an African-American – in the larger society, in my own community, in my own family, and in my own heart.

The legacy of slavery and segregation is indelible in American history. African-Americans also use color to classify, judge, and exclude each other. The fretting over darkness and light in the delivery room happens at ninety percent of the births to African-Americans in my twenty-two-year practice as an obstetrician. Excellent health is not enough. Shade is the obsession. So begins the inadvertent degrading of our children's self-image and self-worth, minimizing our links to their proud African past. Nothing like this happens to white babies. No one cares what shade of white they are or will become. Black and white couples alike share hopes and dreams for family growth and generational success; they all vow to provide whatever the child needs for social, financial, and spiritual flourishing. Only black parents worry about how their child's color will challenge them in America and many other countries that continue to denigrate the experience of black folks. They unanimously perceive the lighter the better, as if repeating the Doll Test that demonstrated the psychological devastation of segregation to the Supreme Court in the year I was born. (In the test, black children who were given black and white dolls said the white dolls were beautiful and the black dolls were ugly.) The society around them gives them good reason for fear.

After a lifetime of promoting the health of women, advocating for equal rights through the Civil Rights Movement and beyond, and bringing up three African-American sons to thrive in this society, I have come face to face with my own learning curves and calls to grow. One of my sons married an ebony descendant of Ghanaian royalty whose family was wary at first about her joining their legacy to a descendant of American slaves. Another son married a blond, blue-eyed, gun-toting white man from North Dakota. Yet another son married a light-skin African-American woman who used her privileged upbringing to mask her belief that racism doesn't exist in America.

The experience of this full spectrum in my life has revealed both the real effects of taught tribalism and the human power to transcend it with love – spousal, familial, personal. The features that constitute each person's distinct identity are no threat to others. We find rich meaning and purpose in who we are – both individually and together – rather than in who we are not. White skin is no more a threat to my African heritage than gay marriage is a threat to my marriage to my husband. And vice versa.

I am sharing my own story as an African-American Baby Boomer woman, physician, and educator in the hopes that my experience will empower others to embrace the color of their skin, the dreams of their hearts, and the unity of the human race where, as the Roman playwright Terence said, "Nothing human is alien to me."

Narrating my life's journey has been both cathartic and illuminating. It recalls the challenges and triumphs I experienced across decades of political turmoil, racism and racial justice (and injustice), the Civil Rights Movement, the women's movement, and affirmative action. It explores the impact on my life's choices of the sexual revolution and the drug explosion in the black community. It highlights my search for identity through revealing family secrets and establishing my legacy.

It is a gift to all, especially women, who question their self-worth, intellectual prowess, and value to others despite their academic and economic success, who feel like outsiders and misfits, who suffer the double consciousness that perpetuates the imposter syndrome, who find themselves vulnerable and constantly seeking validation. As I completed this manuscript, Senator Kamala Harris was nominated to become vice president of the United States. The elevation of Black woman to such a position in our nation is an inspiration and validation for all of us who seek lasting change and justice in our society.

I don't recall awaking any day without thinking of my blackness. Through my journey, my blackness has transformed from a stigma to a badge of honor and beauty, a visible sign of strength, passion, and the legacy of all who have come before me. These are the people and places, the hopes and fears, the light and the darkness that became my path to self-realization, self-worth, self-actualization, and commitment to total wellness for myself as a black – not light– woman and for everyone else. I offer it to illumine your path as well. I challenge my readers to open their hearts and explore the complex colors of your own heart. The places where we find the toxic events as well as the unconditional love imparted by whites and others in America that derail and dehumanize or uplift and empower. There are no solutions here, only a close look at one family, my family, that has navigated this complex terrain.

PART 1
EARLY YEARS

THE PAST

History cannot give us a program for the future, but it can give us a fuller understanding of ourselves and of our common humanity, so that we can better face the future.
~ ROBERT PENN WARREN

Humanity and every individual in it are the products of biology and history, of nature and nurture, of birth and death, of continuity and change, of sex and, one hopes, of love. Biology provides more compelling evidence of our unity than you might expect from the history of how humans have treated one another. In search of my own legacy, I had a DNA test performed that revealed forebears from Africa to the Caucasus.

Seventy-five percent of my ancestors are from Africa – seventeen percent from Cameroon/Congo, fourteen percent from Nigeria, twelve percent, from Ivory Coast, nine percent each from Senegal and Benin/Toto, and seven percent from Mali. These include nations from which African slaves were shipped to Virginia. Specifically, my maternal African ancestry proudly places me as a descendant of the Djola and Fula people of Guinea-Bissau, a West African nation between Senegal on the north and Guinea on the southeast. Their motto, in the native Upper Guinea Creole language, is *Uindade, Luta, Progresso* – "*Unity, Struggle, Progress.*" In addition, nine percent of my ancestors are from the Iberian Peninsula, four percent each from Western Europe and Great Britain, one percent from Italy/Greece, less than one percent from Polynesia, and less than one-tenth of one percent from the Caucasus.

MY MOTHER'S SIDE

The European element came as no surprise. My maternal family had known for years that we were descendants of Admiral Sidney Smith Lee, born in 1802, the eldest brother of Robert E. Lee. Admiral Smith Lee fought with his brother at the Battle of Veracruz during the Mexican-American War and became an officer in the Confederate States Navy. In addition to four sons, including Virginia Governor Fitzhugh Lee, with his wife Anne Marie Mason, he fathered Great-Great-Grandfather William Lee with a slave on the Trout family plantation. William Lee, who was born on April 9, 1839, lived on the Custis family's seventeenth-century White House plantation in New Kent County on the Pamunkey River. John Custis' son Daniel married Martha Dandridge, who was widowed and married George Washington – they owned some two hundred seventy-seven adult slaves.

William Lee's mother's name is unknown – I think of her as "Margarite" and imagine that her parents were captured and shipped from West Africa to Virginia. He married Sarah King, who was born on Feb-

ruary 21, 1845, the daughter of Joe King. Freed slaves
founded the village of Kingston, named for Joe King,
in 1870 on nineteen acres he had purchased. To this
day, the founders and my ancestors are buried at the
village's Ebenezer Baptist Church. William, a farmer,
and Sarah, a teacher, produced eleven children –
Lucious, Andrew, Mary, Willie, Laura, Eliza, Emma,
Alice (Molly), Anna, Charles, and my great-grandfather,
Edward Lee. William died on April 22, 1909, and Sarah
died a few months later, on October 27. Edward Lee
had a daughter, Josephine Lee, my grandmother, with
a beautiful mixed-race woman named Elizabeth Carter.
Elizabeth married Joe Richmond; when he died, she
married a Mr. Wheeler, a widower with two children,
and they had Elizabeth – my "Aunt Lizzy," Josephine's
half-sister. Later, Elizabeth married William's brother
Lucious and became Josephine's aunt, a tangling of the
family line not uncommon in slavery days when families were separated and sold.

Grandma Wheeler became a business owner in
Pittsburgh. The E.H. Wheeler Company which man-
aged domestic workers and ran a local boarding house.
They migrated to Roanoke north to Pennsylvania and
Ohio

Grandmother Josephine married Herbert Lee
Minnis, a commercial window washer, and lived in
Pittsburgh, where they had four children. My mother,
Beatrice Martha Minnis, was the third, born on March
7, 1934. She had an older brother, Beverly; a sister,
Mary Betita; and a younger brother, Joseph. They
moved to Uniontown, Pennsylvania.

MY FATHER'S SIDE

Daddy stood five feet seven inches tall, a thin, muscular man with chocolate mocha- colored skin and callused hands. He was born Wilbert Lee Larkin, along with his twin, Beatrice, in 1928 in Fairmont, West Virginia. His father, Grandpa Wilbert Larkin, was from Yazoo City, Mississippi, but we know little of his family. A feud among some Larkin ancestors had led Wilbert's branch to drop the "s," but Daddy restored it, complicating the world for family genealogists for generations. Daddy also changed his first name from Wilbert to Wilbur.

Grandpa Larkin had migrated to West Virginia to work in the coal mining industry, seeking a better life for his family like many African-American men in those days. He worked in the Fairmont Mining Co.'s No. 8 mine that had reopened after the worst U.S. mining disaster in history in 1907. He sometimes walked seven miles each way so he could support his family. Wilbert Larkin married Viola Cooper, whose family had moved from Bessemer, Alabama, when she was fifteen years old.

Viola's father, born William Metcalf in Tupelo, Mississippi, was a tall, light-skinned man of Haitian descent. He changed his name to Cooper after a family dispute. (I learned as an adult that the Metcalf name came down on the distaff side, despite my parents' invention of a Great-great-grandfather Metcalf.) William married a woman named Jane and had four daughters – Grandma Viola Metcalf/Cooper and her sisters, Aunt Ned and Aunt Bee, who lived in Little Washington, Pennsylvania, and Aunt Icy, who lived in Pittsburgh.

William and Viola had eleven children – my daddy Wilbert, William, James, Milton, Walter, Richard, Melvin, Thelma, Edna, Beatrice, and Pinkey, who died at age seven after a choking accident. They were a close-knit family. As children we spent summers in the county side of Donora, Pennsylvania, where we played from sunup to sundown with very few chores or rules. In 1937, Grandpa William died of pneumonia at age 39, and Grandma Viola married Benjamin Thomas. He was a large, dark-skinned coal miner six feet two inches tall and the only father Daddy knew, and he was kind to Daddy and Grandma. I saw him at Grandma Viola's funeral – in an orange prison suit with his ankles and hands shackled, guarded by two armed State Marshals. He was serving life in prison for murdering a man who disrespected him in public, a flash of a temper that was never directed at his family. I considered his choice to bear the shame of appearing at the funeral a sign of his unconditional love for Viola.

I knew Daddy as a happy, hardworking man who loved his family. He wasn't around as much as I would have liked, but when he was, I knew everything was going to be all right. He was a hero to me. He taught us so much about the world. Although he spoke frankly of world events, it was always in the context of change – hopeful change, inevitable change, future change, quiet change – all through the eyes of a man who spoke of faith as a living, breathing thing.

Daddy loved music of all kinds but favored jazz and blues over any of the ballads popular during his time. I can envision him and Mom dancing together, wrapped in each other's arms as if they didn't have a care in the world. Poor in money but rich in humility, empathy, and parenting, they appear in my memory today as the source of my own servant-leadership. Like all men in my life, he loved cars and drove a Mercury Marquis that was as big as life itself. We would pile in with our picnic basket full of chicken, potato salad, and cold drinks heading toward what felt to us like adventures of a lifetime. From Uniontown to Pittsburgh to McKeesport, Connellsville, and Fairmont, West Virginia, we enjoyed family singa-longs as we rode. We sang in harmony and sometimes out of tune, learning songs from gospel, religious, and secular sources that always focused on love and welcom-ing change. Such soulful melodies would stay with us our entire lives. Through song, we learned the reality of love as well as pain – that dreams of happiness and prosperity can come true. Sam Cook, Diana Ross and the Supremes, New Birth, and the Temptations were part of our every-day lives. Songs are now a blessed memory of the life that gives direction, purpose, and drive to me today.

Daddy was a spiritual soul, always able to move beyond his pain to relieve the pain of others. I remember when he lost two fingers while working at a steel mill in Pittsburgh – he reassured us that he still had enough to get his work done. He danced with us, rarely disciplined us, and provided the breath of fresh air that was enough to encourage us to move on and be better. I don't remember his missing a single day of work. He was a man without pretense. He would invite people who were hungry home for dinner while he enjoyed mashed potato sandwiches. Aunt Edna, who turned ninety in 2020, recalled Daddy's kindness and unlimited care for others in their childhood, especially the many days he came home after a long day in the coal mines with half his sandwich for her, his baby sister. He empowered us to visualize a world where black folks matter, where their American dream is within reach.

Daddy graduated from high school while working part-time in the coal mines from age fifteen then served in the U.S. Army, inspired by the Tuskegee Airmen. He returned home with hopes of racial equality in the land of the free – hopes never realized – and met Beatrice Martha (Mareta) Minnis.

GROWING UP

I grew up in the coal towns around Pittsburgh with the usual focus on family, strict rules, and church. My early years were in rural communities where we raised our own food, lacked indoor plumbing, and swam in the reservoir. When Daddy's job switched from coal to steel, we moved to "the projects," a high-rise in a more urban setting with supermarket jobs, indoor plumbing, and lots more people around. Finally, he took a second job and was able to buy a house for us in town. These experiences – changing friends, changing schools, changing cultures – came with challenges but prepared me for a life of dealing with change.

LEMONT FURNACE

We lived in Lemont Furnace, a township three miles northeast of Uniontown, forty-six miles southeast of Pittsburgh, and fifty-five miles northeast of Fairmont, West Virginia, where my father was born and where he commuted to work in the coal mines. Lemont Furnace was one many towns where coal was burned to make coke then shipped to the steel mills Pittsburgh and nearby states.

I imagine he cared little about what his coworkers, managers, or even his black friends thought of him as a short, dark-skinned man. He was a man of God. He would tell us his journey to find God's footprint for him and taught us to learn more about the God that had led him through the Kingdom Hall, the Catholic Church, Islam, and the Baptist congregation where we settled.

Life in Lemont Furnace was organized around family, church, school, play, and chores. We had plenty of relatives to celebrate holidays and show up at funerals. They taught us how to navigate being black in America. We were forbidden to speak in the presence of adults. I would hide or sit quietly listening to stories of triumph, promotions, disrespect, or maltreatment at the hands of white employers and co-workers or black colleagues. These stories were always the same: white employers who showed little appreciation for hard work, white coworkers who enjoyed flaunting white privilege, or black co-workers who were supportive, fearful, or hostile. I learned always to study folks around me before letting them see into my heart and soul. I learned to fear the ever-present danger of losing your livelihood, being misjudged, or being excluded from a well-earned opportunity. These fears and threats were real for both whites and blacks. I should have listened and embraced the wisdom. Across the years, I wound up in many situations I was taught to avoid.

Almost all my family members lived in two-parent households where mothers did not work outside the home unless they were cleaning others' houses. Momma was the typical parent who keep our house and clothes clean, monitored our school activities, made home-cooked meals every day, and disciplined us so we would grow up to be "acceptable citizens." I didn't know what she meant until much later in life. Being a Negro child born in the fifties meant the pitfalls of failure outnumbered many of the carefully planned opportunities our parents hoped would lead us to success and prosperity. It meant avoiding getting too close to white folks who might prove untrustworthy. It meant never placing ourselves in a position of danger or the appearance of wrongdoing. It meant few friends and minimal social activities.

Church was my social outlet. Mt. Rose Baptist Church in Uniontown was everything a young girl could want – bobbing for apples during Halloween, Christmas plays and Easter pageants, mother-daughter teas and summer picnics. Sundays were for dressing up, repenting, eating, relaxing with family, and listening to the radio. My friends and I spent weekends together participating in a majorette team. The Christianity there felt both uplifting and punishing – I was confused. I later revisited religion, a major turning point in my life.

Lemont Furnace and Uniontown were safe places for our family through the early years of the Civil Rights Movement. We lived a simple life, killing chickens and rabbits for food, content with outhouses and well water. Saturday night baths in a small tin tub were a family affair – we shared one another's bath water, a custom in homes with little water and less ability to heat it. The reservoir was the neighborhood pool. Lost lives of playmates who drowned in the deep waters were regrettable facts of life – most public pools were off-limits to black people, so few of us knew how to swim. Holidays meant playtime with cousins and constant discipline from adults who warned us not to eavesdrop on grown-up conversations. "Little pitchers have big ears," they would say to guard the family secrets.

MCKEESPORT

In 1962, Daddy got a job in the steel mill and we moved from the tranquil countryside of Uniontown to a three-bedroom apartment on the eighth floor of a high-rise in Harrison Village, a low-income housing development overlooking the Monongahela River in McKeesport near my elementary school. These were the infamous "projects," a place where folks of color could be easily contained. We were excited to get out of the car when Daddy pulled into the parking lot – a crowd yelling nearby sounded like a carnival. As we rushed over, we saw blood streaming down the faces of two men who had resorted to violence to settle a dispute.

The novelty of a new home for us children was a traumatic experience for my Mom. The indoor plumbing instead of outhouses, the supermarkets instead of butchering, the bus rides instead of long walks could not outweigh her fears. She had no friends, no relatives, no roots in McKeesport, and she was trying to raise four young children. I remember being an ordinary kid with no school friends. My siblings were my friends.

Every night, my mom would make us come home before dark, and we would sit on the porch watching other kids play in the park below. Mom kept us very close. We didn't have the experience of forming friendships through play dates. We didn't go to the park. We weren't allowed to participate in after-school activities. We were supposed to be my mother's friends – after all, she was only fifteen years old when she had her first child. She wanted us around all the time. I didn't have the opportunity to form "normal" childhood friendship bonds.

Once I was playing outside with my first white friend in McKeesport when her mother called her in. The girl protested that she wanted to play longer with her new friend, and her mother said: "You are not to play with her, ever. She is not your friend. She's a colored girl." The sting of those words is forever etched in my memory. Color was a disease, not just a difference. I had one true black playmate, Tracy, an only child, who lived close to my floor in the projects. Mom let us stay overnight at each other's houses once in a while. Tracy was my best friend through high school. She was what they called "high yellow," with full lips and an infectious laugh. I don't know whether she had other friends – we were together most of the time on this life journey. The gossips said her relatives ran and staffed a nearby brothel. I visited these beautiful women with gorgeous hairstyles and makeup who wore filmy, see-through, flowing clothing that screamed: "Beautiful body! Yes, I am a woman!" To me, they were beautiful inside as well as out. They were kind and gentle, always encouraging me to make something of myself. They supported each other in a taboo profession and always found time to tell this little black girl she was special.

All of Momma's lessons were "be a good girl," "what you do in the dark will eventually come to light," "God sees your every move" – all to frighten us away from sex, drugs, and alcohol – never a conversation about birth control, education, careers, or intimacy. It didn't work: two of her girls, like her, got pregnant as teenagers. We were subjected to physical, psychological, emotional, and social abuse from neighbors and church going folks. Isolation from the community at large had a profound impact on our self-worth, self-image, and self-empowerment. We received little forgiveness or nurturing, but moderate doses of anger and disappointment.

NORTH VERSAILLES

When I was in high school, Daddy got a second job so he could afford to buy a house for us in North Versailles. He devoted his life to making our lives better. He worshipped my mom. He was her chauffeur, her banker, her friend, and her confidant, but he could not fulfill the Cinderella complex she harbored – a knight in shining armor with plenty of money to rescue her from poverty, defend her honor, and give her a house with a white picket fence around the yard where her children would play as they grew old together – a dream many women share. Instead, she had to pinch pennies to feed and clothe her children with little left for herself.

Because we were still poor, living from paycheck to paycheck, Christmas meant one gift for each child. We could ask for anything, but we usually went for necessities – maybe a sweater or a skirt so we would have an extra change of clothes. When I was sixteen, I decided I wanted a pair of white go-go boots, the rage at the time. I had seen them on TV worn by many thin, blond-haired white women. My mother objected that they were impractical – winter was cold in Pennsylvania, and they would not keep me warm – but I begged. Sure enough, the go-go boots were under the Christmas tree, and I screamed for joy. I was so proud to wear them to my friend's party that day. I was freezing in those boots, but I was so happy. I came home, and Momma asked how it went with the boots. I told her how much people loved them, how pretty they were on me.

"They're not warm, Mom," I admitted. She lit into me about wants versus needs, about trying to please others, trying to be cute, and all these things that I was not. She also told me that white people could tolerate cold weather better than blacks because our ancestors were acclimated to warmer climates in Africa. I accepted that and still think about it when I find myself bundling up and whining about cold that doesn't bother my white colleagues. I left that conversation still happy I got the go-go boots. For that Christmas moment in time, I let myself feel loved by her anyway.

The friction with Momma stemmed from the teaching of her mother, Grandma Josephine. I remember her as a sad woman who constantly complained that she had married beneath her station. She enjoyed friends and family but never displayed love for Grandfather Herbert. He was so light-skinned he could pass "when it mattered," as Grandma said, but failed to leverage that "light" privilege to elevate his family's place in the white world. In her eyes, their shade and our "good hair" proved that our slave ancestors were house workers, not field hands. She proudly reported that she had worked in the White House as a trusted switchboard operator because of her lighter skin. She had also landed a prestigious job as a domestic for the Jewish Goldman family. Grandma impressed upon us that keeping a clean house was the path to self-actualization – never put your feet on furniture, chew with your mouth closed, elbows off the table, and never, ever accept a treat at a white person's house. She believed she had advanced as a domestic by putting just the right starch in the white folks' shirts and blouses, the envy of her fellow domestics, and cooking the meals they enjoyed. Proper etiquette would make us stand out as good Negroes.

We were warned not to associate with darker people — "they will never fade on me," Grandma said. Also never date a dark man — a standing disrespect for my dark-skinned father — because jobs and wealth come easier the lighter and closer to the white race you are. Momma's fatal error of marrying a darker man she happened to love, consigned to coal mine and steel mill jobs because of his shade, was the source of countless I-told-you-so's from her relatives.

Now I understand that Grandma's bias was a learned behavior considered vital for her survival in a world where race and color dictated how well you could feed and educate your family. The practice of "passing" was common because it meant a chance at white privilege that continues to elude people of color. Tension endures in some quarters between dark- and light-skinned blacks today because of this history. Grandma Minnis really loved us and wanted only to protect us from the many shades of darkness that still haunt the lives of African-Americans today.

Momma also did her best to prepare us for black life in America. If we came from school confused about something unfair, she turned it into a life lesson. One day in elementary school when we were leaving class, the teacher turned around and said, "Many of you don't have your books in your hands, and you have assignments. March back in that classroom." I was sitting there, one of two black students, watching others slide their books from underneath their desks, so I reached to do the same. The teacher yelled, "Margaret!" that meant she was mad — everyone called me Delarese or Dela. I told her I was getting my book to take home. She said, "No, you were getting your book because you knew if you didn't have your book, you were going to be punished." She called me to the front of the class, lectured me on dishonesty, and hit me with the ruler. When I told Mamma, she said it was dishonest to try that, but she added: "The reason you were caught is because your hand was black." Putting my hand on a white piece of paper, she said, "This is what most of your classmates look like, and they all blend in, but you don't. That's what people see first when they see you, the color of your skin."

My parents lived through the Great Migration of African-Americans moving north and the Tuskegee Study of Untreated Syphilis in the Negro Male resulting in the early death of their wives and the birth of deformed children. They also witnessed the Olympic triumphs of Jesse Owens, Harry Truman's desegregation of the military, the Nobel Peace Prize awarded to Dr. Ralph Bunche, the *Brown v. Board* Supreme Court decision, and the murders of Medgar Evers, Emmitt Till, John Kennedy, Robert Kennedy, Martin Luther King Jr., and Malcolm X.

I got a glimpse of Momma's perspective on the Civil Rights Movement in the spring of 1968 when I came home for lunch. The food was on the table, but she was in front of the television where Walter Cronkite was announcing that Robert F. Kennedy had been shot. Momma was pale and weeping. For the first time, I grasped how much I didn't know about the world. I didn't know what this white man meant to people of color, the hope they saw in him, until I saw my mother cry. Then I cried.

After the assassination of Dr. Martin Luther King Jr., I had started to see many tears shed over folks we knew only by their passion for folks of color and the risks they took to make things right. This triggered an anger toward white people I couldn't explain. Good white folks like Kennedy had been killed by white folks. I saw the destructive power of bias. I was driving down the street in McKeesport with friends when three white teenager girls pulled up beside us. They rolled down the windows and called us "nigger bitches." I was so angry that I forgot all the good white people in my life. They sped off, and I chased them. We were side by side at the next stoplight. They were laughing. I got out of the car and yelled at them: "Yes, this black bitch will put you six feet under!" It was so horrible. I was angry and more violent than I imagined possible. It even frightened me. It was as if these girls had killed Martin Luther King themselves. Anyone in that space who was not an African-American was not on my side. I went to marches, became an activist, appreciated Malcolm X, and even considered joining the Nation of Islam in my efforts to understand the society that was killing my people and people who cared about us. All I saw were broken promises and hatred.

Around this time, my friendship with a schoolmate, Doris, started blossoming. I was drawn to her because she was popular, outspoken, and fearless. She was not the good girl my momma wanted me to befriend. Her family was considered violent because they met violence with violence. Fights and antagonism followed her everywhere. I was a frequent target of bullying. Kids would follow me home, hitting me, pulling my hair, and threatening me. I was afraid to fight back. I had one fight in middle school and one in high school. Doris pushed me into fighting back because it was her culture, part of developing your own brand as someone with grit and a regular pastime. We often gathered around to watch people fight.

Doris was a strong figure in my life for a long time, but in high school, I realized we weren't really friends. She talked about me behind my back. Shed put me on the spot to do things like dancing in public that was hard for me – her encouragement was fake. I was bullied all through high school because I wouldn't fight. Doris was a kingpin. If she said don't touch me, they wouldn't touch me. Sometimes she would protect me, maybe because she thought I couldn't defend myself.

My brother Herb became my savior through late middle school and high school. Other girls were getting gang-raped; no one would touch me. In the impoverished community known as the ghetto, we were surrounded by predators. The white candy store owner tried to lure me into his basement where I am sure other young girls had been violated. A man touched my breast in the restroom of a local black owned restaurant – my father found him and defended my honor. I saw people shot and killed in the street.

Having entered puberty, finding love was paramount for all my friends. My first boyfriend, "Pint," was very popular, a gorgeous guy. He was tall and thin with dark, wavy good hair. I often thought he was a black Mexican. He probably had lots of girlfriends. I was fifteen years old. He was around nineteen, owned a motorcycle, and would take me riding. I didn't lose virginity with him. I was saying "no" all the time – "I'm not ready." I got into a vicious cycle of beatings from him, but I was used to this. I lived in a household where it was the norm.

I was much older before I realized that beatings from those who claim to love you should not be normal. I advocate now for women who are victims of intimate partner violence, but I have not been a powerful force. Even at my age, I have not resolved my own allowing myself to be subjected to such violence in the name of love. It still happens to women today. I tolerated it. I didn't tell people. I thought I needed a beating because I had been beaten so much, because I wasn't behaving well. I wasn't quite good enough. If he loved me, why would he hurt me? Maybe I wasn't pretty enough, smart enough. What did I do wrong? I was trained with a cycle of beatings from loved ones, starting with my mom.

Pint ridiculed and beat me often in public, but with him and his motorcycle, I could sneak away from my parents and do all those things we were not supposed to do – leave my community after dark, hang with an older crowd – so I tolerated him. One night we met under the streetlight on a corner near my house. I didn't know my father was watching. Pint started hitting me and yelling at me, and my father stormed out from the shadows toward us.

He confronted Pint, telling him to never to put his hands on me again. He was trying to protect me. I marveled that the person I saw the least would defend me. Did he really know me? Why did he think I was worth defending? I always saw my daddy as the good guy, the protector, the one who would save me, whereas I saw my mother as trying to crush me. Pint ultimately died on his motorcycle – he wasn't wearing a helmet when he ran into a pole. That is my lasting memory of him.

Roy was the second love of my life, and the father of my first child – it happened on the first or second encounter. That complicated my life and validates my mom's opinion of me. She continued to find ways to punish me.

I didn't have to tell my mom I was pregnant. She was counting feminine pads and keeping up with my menstrual cycles. She confronted me: "You didn't have a period this month." We didn't go to the doctor to get a pregnancy test. She started mixing concoctions to help me abort – Black Beauties, another name for amphetamines, and a formula from her past that I had to drink every day. I didn't lose my baby, so I carried him to term. She wasn't loving, but she didn't hit me, and she helped me get ready for the baby. I was scared, but I wanted to this right. I needed to do everything right for the rest of my life, to plan well because my baby would depend on me. I wanted to be the best mother I could be.

I was sixteen years old. I was studious but didn't feel smart. I must have gotten good grades because I went on to college. All our lives, we were forced to get it done. If you had a project, you got it done, and you got it done well – read, prepare for tests, stay close to home, study, do what you had to do. The teachers were always right, even when I suspected that they were belittling and ignoring me. Momma would make excuses for the teachers, making me feel devalued by both of them.

A few bright moments came from those I least expected. I was about twenty weeks pregnant and just beginning to show when I went to school one day wearing my first stylish maternity top. None of the teachers had noticed. My English teacher, Mr. Lewis, a young white man, was shocked when he saw me and exclaimed in front of the class: "No, not you!" I sensed his disappointment. He talked about how well I was doing, how much potential I had – I was a great writer, a great student. He saw this little black girl, now pregnant, who would never ever have an opportunity to amount to anything. I read his disappointment in his face. He saw more potential in me than I saw in myself. Recovering from that awkward outburst, he lectured on how bumps the road can enhance our growth and not hold us back. That white man said I could be great. That was powerful – one of those unexpected blessings my father often promised. I had never believed I could be significant.

Graduation was coming. McKeesport High School had more than eight hundred students but few African-Americans. I remember no black teacher except the football coach, but I never felt treated differently, maybe because the racism was systemic and hidden. I knew my counseling was sometimes poor, but I didn't blame bias until later when I realized their assumption that I would never be a medical professional. My counselors would say, "What kind of a trade are you going to do?" "I think I want to be a nurse." "No, no, you need to learn a trade, take home economic classes." I was bad at that. They were not steering me toward a professional position. Out of the whole school, only a few African-Americans attended college, and only two attended medical school. I believe we had those dreams counseled out of us.

During high school, I dreamed of being a cheerleader. I worked hard, learned the cheers, and had a baby. I went back to try again, and after tryouts I was confident I would make the squad. Then the teacher/coach pulled me aside and said I couldn't be a cheerleader because I had a baby and was not a good role model. I was shocked but too quiet to defend myself, too insecure to challenge. I complained to Mamma that I had no chance because I had a baby. She asked; Has there ever been an African-American cheerleader on that squad? I wondered: Was it my race, my baby, or both?

Except for the gossip, especially at church with its constant reminders of my sin and shame, the pregnancy was uneventful. Dr. Lanauze was a community general practitioner of Puerto Rican descent. We honored him as a physician of color who, as Booker T. Washington said, had dropped his bucket and devoted his life to our community. He cared for everyone – chronic disease, acute disease, women, men, and children. He welcomed us all. My pregnancy was by all measures normal for a sixteen-year-old. The nurses were not kind, but not mean. They were detached from me and this birth. I tried to detach myself too, but I suffered the self-inflicted trauma of believing I was not good enough. I went into labor experiencing the pain and fear of any sixteen-year-old child unprepared for childbirth. I tried not to scream or yell for fear of embarrassing my parents. The pain was horrible. I thought I would die. I was alone. My mother wasn't allowed to be with me. No one was there to reassure me that everything would be OK. I don't know whether fathers were permitted, but this was not an option. This was no place for Roy, the father of my baby, who had moved on to another naïve classmate. I felt I was near death, but I was told I would be going to sleep. I had general anesthesia and awakened with a beautiful baby boy, Carlos. I loved him from the moment I met him. I was seventeen years old and doing well in school. My classmates or counselors didn't accept that I wanted to go to college, but I was determined.

I joined Future Nurses of America, and a young recruiter, Chenits Pettigrew, came to tell us about a new opportunity at the University of Pittsburgh for African-American girls – an on-campus summer program after high school that would get you accepted into the nursing program if you earned a C or higher in your science courses. It was an affirmative-action program to level the playing field and fully integrate the nursing school. I believed there was equal talent but not equal opportunity. About two dozen girls came from all over – D.C., Philadelphia, Baltimore – and almost all of us got into the program.

MY PARENTS

Momma stood five feet five inches tall with a petite, curvy body; a large bust; light skin; and long, dark, reddish-brown hair. Daddy chose her over a young German woman he had dated during his service shortly after World War II. They married when she was fifteen years old and he was twenty-two. She gave birth to Mary Elizabeth at sixteen, Herbert at eighteen, me at twenty, and Faith Annette at twenty-five. She told me without emotion that I was born on a warm day in June, the birth month of many people in our family, after an uneventful pregnancy and delivery at segregated Uniontown Hospital where black babies had a better chance at survival.

I often think of Daddy as the coal miner and often refer to myself as the coal miner's daughter. I wonder what he was thinking as he loaded into the shaft that took him miles underground to a cold, damp darkness so he could provide for his family.

MOMMA'S BEATINGS: FEAR, LOVE, AND DISCIPLINE

I can't remember any time in my life when I wasn't threatened with beatings. All of us were beaten to some degree. I felt I was the target of beatings for just being me. I felt that she was beating me not only physically — she was beating out

24

of me any ounce of hope of who I could possibly be beyond a baby who was just about to have a baby. She was instilling guilt and making me believe I would never be good enough or pretty enough.

The beatings started when I was so young I can't remember the age. Maybe they started as a slap on the back or a slap on the face. They escalated fast. That was the culture in many African-American families, with frequent reference to Proverbs 13:24: "You spare the rod, you spoil the child." I can't remember a time I was not afraid of being beaten, usually with a hand or a belt. Early on, it was several tree switches, soon followed by whatever was handy and always accompanied by a tongue-lashing. Sometimes it was a hard-soled shoe. I was beaten for anything mom thought wasn't perfect. I was constantly trying to please her. When I was washing dishes, if there was one she deemed not clean enough, she would haul off and hit me with her hand. When I was outside playing and she called me in, no matter how fast I arrived, if it was later than she expected, she would hit me with a belt. When I went out with friends, if I came home a few minutes late or hadn't told her everywhere I was going, she beat me. It was overwhelming. My memories are full of running away from her and her belts, scrambling under the dining room table to avoid the strap, her vicious approach any way she could reach me. I knew only that she would beat me for any wrongdoing she perceived.

One rare exception came when I had an accident riding my bicycle on Whigham Street where we lived. I flipped over the handlebars, landed on a car, broke my collarbone, and went to the hospital to get a cast. She didn't hit me for days after that, maybe because she figured I was in enough pain. Then one day when she came home and found my sisters and me on the porch, she flew into a rage because we hadn't done our chores. She was so angry she slapped me on the back – forgetting about my cast. She hurt her hand so much she started crying. My unspoken reaction was: "See how it hurts when you get hit!" I was happy she hurt because of all the pain we had felt over the years. Then I felt so guilty for that. I remember praying about it because I delighted in her pain.

We all had our share of beatings, but as the middle child, I felt especially targeted. One day when I was twelve, I was ironing, a chore with strict rules about pressing and folding, and I was in a hurry to go out and play. I decided to save time by folding the blouses first, then ironing just the front and back. My sister noticed and tattled. Momma came in and said, "What a great job" – then suddenly unfolded one to reveal the wrinkles inside. She yelled at me, called me a deceitful liar, beat me with the belt, threw all the blouses back into the basket, and made me start over. I lost my playtime for another day.

Momma also beat me every time I wet the bed, sometimes five times a week. It was a ritual: you wet the bed, you clean the sheets, you get a beating. Sometimes the beatings came after school.

I wasn't alone in this. Bedwetting happened so often in my household that my brother, my sisters, and I thought it was normal. Herb, the pride and joy of the Larkins' clan, was perfect in every way – except he wet the bed too. But the taunting and threats after a night of wet bed sheets and scrubbing stains out of mattresses never seemed to faze him. After one of these cold, wet events, Momma put him in a dress and tied him to the clotheslines in the backyard. He could run and play only from one end of the line to the other, pole to pole. We made it part of our game. I marveled at how he managed to fill such terrible situations with imagination and wonder. I learned later that he faked nonchalance – inside, he was embarrassed and horrified.

Living in a drafty home proved a challenge beyond imagination. Sleeping together was a family togetherness forced by poverty. If one of us wet the bed, all three of us slept in a wet bed. The worst were the winter nights when we had to sleep with our coats. Wearing urine-soaked coats to school the next day made us targets for bullying and ridicule.

I was always proud of myself when I awoke to find a dry bed, happy not to face a belt whipping or lose time with my friends. I was getting older and hoping that I would "grow out of it" in time for the junior prom. I wet the bed until I was thirteen, but my shame grew in middle school and I sought to hide it from my friends.

Momma wouldn't let that happen. I wet the bed on Friday night and knew I wouldn't be allowed to go to the Saturday noon football game -- my beloved McKeesport Tigers versus the East Allegheny Wildcats. Unexpectedly, my friends showed up at my house to walk with me to the stadium. I said I couldn't go. Momma took me aside and offered an exception – if I would accept a beating while they waited. Faced with yet another display of her cold heart, I resolved to show her I could take her beatings, I had grown numb to this pain. She delivered the worst beating I had ever got for bedwetting. I wet myself while she was beating me, but I never cried out. When it ended, I cleaned up, changed my clothes, joined my friends, and went to the game.

After that, I never looked at my mother the same. I loved her. She was my mother. But I clearly saw the cold heart of the mother I longed to love unconditionally. The physical pain of the constant beatings faded quickly, but the emotional pain of the beatings endured through my life. It taught me to beat my own son for petty things like candy wrappers on the floor, advancing the abuse to another generation.

The cycle continued until my husband Chenits and I moved to California when my son Carlos was eight, and I became a mother who learned to discipline with love and patience. Chenits, an only child, had never been hit by his parents. He considered it a cruel and barbaric way to teach a child right from wrong. I saw the pain on his face when I hit Carlos, a child he loved from the day they met. One day, I said, "No more. This cannot be part of my legacy with this man, my husband, who had never been hit by his mother." He was such a gentle spirit and such a wonderful person. I said, "Beating is not the way I can help this child be the best he can be." I took a long time to see what beatings had done to me. I was still that scared little girl who only wanted to be loved and nurtured. Carlos was also a bed wetter, but he stopped soon after the beatings stopped. Had he grown out of it? Did the beatings exacerbate the bedwetting? When I stopped beating him, I felt these decades-long episodes end in my own life, although I believe those childhood experiences contributed to my own psychological and social challenges and lack of self-worth and self-esteem. As a physician I often wonder if this represented the ACES (Adverse Childhood experiences) that affect many black children disproportionately.

It wasn't just the beatings. I never felt loved by my mother throughout my childhood. I thought she would treat me better if I could do things to make her happy, but I never succeeded. I have no memory of owning or playing with dolls. No imaginary tea parties or make-believe houseguests. My sisters remember dolls in the house, but we were poor, and none of them belonged just to me. I spent much of my time reading old books, counting trains and automobiles, or talking with my siblings.

I was in my early 40s when I told my mom and siblings how I felt. They started buying me unique dolls, and now I have a beautiful collection. A few years ago, Aunt Barbara gave me one of her dolls, and the memory warms me whenever I see it. I enjoy sharing dolls with adults as well as children. Someday I'd like to start a nonprofit to give dolls to children in the same circumstances – Dolls from Dela.

I have no memory of a birthday party until I turned sixteen. I was reluctant to have friends over because of my mom's erratic behavior – she could switch without warning from sweet and tender to angry and cold. Her behavior would likely be diagnosed as manic-depressive disorder today. She agreed to let me host my sixteenth birthday party, and I was excited beyond belief to plan it. I was going to have my school friends over for the first time, and we would have a great time dancing in the basement.

It wasn't fun. I felt like I was just trying to hold myself together, not to be embarrassed in front of my mom. I wanted it over as soon as it started. I resolved to do the opposite with my own children. I celebrated their birthdays almost every single year with abundant joy and plenty of friends and good people. I still consider birthdays and special events as opportunities to make lasting good memories. I wanted to spare my kids my pain. I am trying to give them as many joyful memories as possible.

DADDY'S CARE

My father was the bright light in those dark days of my childhood. He hit me only once in my entire life, and only because Momma demanded it. She told him every day that we were not good children and always misbehaved. One day, she wore him down and declared, "I'm not going to hit her – you're going to hit her." The infraction, as usual, was so petty I don't remember it. He took me to the basement and said, "I have to do this because your mom says I have to do this." I don't remember the beating itself – I just knew that it didn't come from him. It was about his love for Momma, not anger toward me. He was the one who took care of me.

When I was eighteen and started to experiment with marijuana, Daddy invited me to share a joint with him. "You think you're so smart," he said. "If you're going to do this, you need to do it safely. Let's have one of those things together." We smoked and laughed together in the basement he had furnished for himself. I think it was his first time smoking weed – an odd way to teach a lesson, but one I will never forget. "To me, this is not a drug of choice," he said. "I like alcohol. But if you ever do this, you need to do it around people who care about you and will take care of you."

Daddy was kind and giving to anyone he saw in need – money, clothes, a meal. Many nights we ate with strangers he invited because they were hungry. White, black,

Puerto Rican, young, old — they were all welcomed into our home, even though we were so poor that water or milk sometimes counted as treats. I would find Mom in the kitchen trying to figure out how to stretch the food — deciding who would get less so we could feed the unexpected guests. Daddy made us practice kindness toward others. He reassured me that any act of kindness would be returned when we least expected it.

Before long, I experienced one of those returns. One day, a few of my friends and I rode with an older guy to a dance in a little place called Jeannette, almost twenty miles from McKeesport. When the driver wanted to go to another party and we wouldn't join him because it was late, he left us stranded. Close to midnight, we were walking down the road when an older black man pulled over and asked, "What are you doing out this late? Who are your parents? What do your parents do?" "My dad works in the Duquesne Works steel mill," I said. Mr. Hamilton was on his way home from his shift at the same steel mill where my father worked. He told us to get into the car. We obeyed him without fear — unlike today. He drove us all the way home to McKeesport and told us never to travel so far from home again. "It's not safe for girls to be out alone," he said. He did this because he worked in the steel mill with Daddy, but I don't believe he ever told.

BEAUTIFUL TO BE BLACK
BY CHARA NYASHIA SANJO

"It's beautiful to be black."

It is the color of strength and pride.
I will say it out loud. I don't have to hide.
I love me, and the color that I represent.
Look at me, there is nothing like it.
What you see is not an illusion.
It's a gift from GOD, don't ever confuse it.

"It's beautiful to be black."

It is the color of fame and envy.
If I wasn't black, I wouldn't be me.
Black is the color of power and authority.
It is so outstanding, thank you LORD for blessing
me.
I'll shout it to the world, I'm proud of what I am.
Those who are in vain will never understand.

"It's beautiful to be black"

It is the color of confidence and style.
I have been blessed, by my ancestor from the Nile.
I am scenic from the inside out.
These verses are true, I don't have any doubt.
There is no one who can change my mind.
Black has been beautiful since the beginning of
time.

"It's beautiful to be black."

It is the color of honor and grace.
This is one thing that cannot be taken away.

MY SIBLINGS

Four children – my brother, my two sisters, and me – grew up in the family that Daddy and Momma created. I was the third born, after Mary Elizabeth and Herb, before Faith Annette. Growing up, we experienced the usual dynamics of rivalry and bonding, of competition and support. As adults, our relationships continue that complex flow across time. Through each of us, our family has extended and grown – the siblings and their children have brought in spouses, and I have nieces and nephews to the third generation now, each with a unique place in our individual lives and our life as a whole.

HERB

My brother Herb, born after Mary and before me, lived a privileged life, as interpreted by black families, as the only son of the family. The rules that applied to the girls did not apply to him. He was excused with the typical claims of boys. He mocked us with, "I'm rough and tough, and I can get away with things" because my parents believed he was more capable than we were. He was not spared from beatings, especially because he was a bed wetter, but not as often as the girls. Still, he lived in the same household and suffered the same physical and psychological abuse.

Herb and I grew close, often chatting and playing together. The difference between us involved our parents' treatment, especially my mother's because my father was usually away working, sometimes two jobs. Herb had few chores, and he got away with doing them poorly or not at all. But he was kind to me. Around my friends, he was never judgmental and never made me feel small or unworthy of his friendship. I never remember a cross word between us as children. Instead, he tried to include me in many of his activities.

Herb was always nearby when I was out and about. He showed up in the craziest places when I was doing the craziest things. He was always my protector. I considered him the person in my life who really cared about me. He often came to my rescue, beginning when I was about seven years old in Lemont Furnace, where we kept chickens and roosters. Once I was attacked by a rooster that jumped on my head and started pecking. I was screaming and running, but Herb shooed the rooster away. I was forever grateful. Even in such a minor incident, he was one of my few heroes. He made sure I was not ashamed to reach out when I needed help

His heroism saved me when we went to swim at the neighborhood YMCA, a pool where blacks were assigned specific swimming hours. Because African-Americans were often barred from public pools and some had drowned in the reservoir, my friends and I never learned to swim. Foolishly, I jumped into the deep end and started to sink. I swallowed water and suddenly felt at peace, like I was going to die but it was OK. At that moment, I was snatched out of the pool and started vomiting as I gasped for breath. I opened my eyes and saw people standing around me. The lifeguard hadn't noticed me – Herb came to my rescue. When he tells the story, he says, "You were just gone. I didn't see you come back up. I realized you were out there, and I had to snatch you out of there or you were going to be dead." He became the sibling I could always trust, always looking out for me.

Growing up in McKeesport wasn't easy, especially for girls, because there were multiple predators, black and white men who sought to lure middle and high schoolers into unsafe situations. My father always warned me to be safe, always travel in groups. Sometimes a gang of men and boys would corner four or five of us to harass or paw at us. I never got gang-raped, but I saw it happen to my friends. Early on, Herb told a group of young men in my presence: "I don't know what you're up to, but you'd better not put a hand on my sister, ever, or I will kill you." They never touched me. I escaped that brutality because Herb was there to protect me.

As Herb got older, he grew very rebellious, staying out late with his friends. Dad confronted him during high school, and he left our home for part of a summer with a friend, hitchhiking across the country, doing as they pleased, and making their home wherever they felt comfortable. He tells stories of sleeping under bridges or on the side of the road as well as eating Cheetos and chips for dinner. When he came back, he lived with friends, completed high school, joined the Army, and married a slightly older woman, Billie, from McKeesport. When he was stationed in Germany, they had their first son, Eddie. Herb adored my little nephew and talked about him all the time. But he was flirtatious like many military men, and he drank too much. His marriage was struggling, although the military helped him grow up significantly. He learned about leadership and how to be a well-rounded citizen of the world – my mother's goal for all of us. He became very politically motivated to understand what was going on in our society and our world. We talked often about current events, civil rights, and how the nation and the world had dictated "our place." He struggled as a black man in the military, where he served among some overt racists, and in the job market after he was discharged despite his loyal service. He appreciated the white men who had his back and respected him as an equal. The challenge of the colors of his heart was ever-present, just as it was for our father, who served during World War II only to return home to a country that devalued him. Dad got unequal treatment even though he was a proud American-born man who wanted only to live the American dream and take care of his family.

The family returned from Germany, but Herb seemed alone and bitter. Billie and Eddie returned to Germany to start a new life. Today, Eddie is a successful young man, married to a white woman, and I have two beautiful mixed-race granddaughters, Kiara & Tina, whom we adore. Herb and Eddie remain close.

Herb eventually became involved with Condessa, my friend since I was eighteen. Condessa, previously a ward of the court in Philadelphia, had Cuban-African-American ancestry. She and her siblings grew up in foster care. She came to Pittsburgh after Chenits helped her get into college, and we spent a lot of time together especially during holidays. Herb was in a band called Pyramid whose members were very alert to where we came from, our heritage, and our legacy. Their wonderful original music told stories about us as Africans and African-Americans, love ballads and dance music. They became very popular around Pittsburgh and moved to California seeking the big-time in the music industry. Around this time, Herb changed his name to Rahim. Many African-Americans were rebelling against the European-American names given to their slave ancestors. He refused to be called Herb and insisted on the Muslim name, although he later reverted to Herb.

Most of the band became practicing Muslims in Los Angeles, where they got jobs and performed on the side. When Chenits and I decided to move to California, Herb was eager to help us. He found an apartment for us, and I stayed with him when I went ahead of Chenits to find a job. He taught us how to navigate the city and build a life in Los Angeles.

Most of the family hoped that Herb's relationship with Condessa would lead to marriage, but after more than ten years, they separated and he married a woman named Cynthia. We thought that he might have been see-ing her while with Condessa, a suspicion both denied. I didn't want to believe it – that behavior didn't square with the kind brother I knew and loved.

Cynthia was a police officer, quiet and smart, with a gentle spirit, very different from all the other women Herb dated. He maintained his music but became a soil scientist, working for a company to make sure land was suitable for office buildings, railroads, and major industrial projects. He was very good at his job and continues to work in the industry today. He and Cynthia had two children, Herbert Junior and Brian. After Brian was born, they separated but remained friends and parented together.

After some time, Herb reunited with Condessa, who had become a physician. But after about twenty years altogether, they decided they had very little in common and separated. She met someone and became engaged, but they stayed such good friends that Herb helped her pack her wedding dress and accessories for the trip to the church on her wedding day. They're still friends.

Herb, continuing his revolving door, met someone named Linda. I disliked her. She was a bad fit, lacking any common commitment to life, morals, ethics, or goals, so they eventually separated. He eventually met a sweet young woman named Margaret, fell in love, married her, and remains with her today. He focuses on filling his married life with rich family memories.

Herb maintained both his concern for race and world affairs and his engagement with music. A contract with RCA Records for Pyramid fell through years ago, but the group continued to tour. Very talented members would leave and come back, sometimes getting on big circuits with well-known entertainers. Two of them, Jimmy and Sunny, died of AIDS in the mid-1980s. I watched Herb embrace them and love them through this disease. They were his great friends, colleagues, and peers. Almost all of them came from the Pittsburgh-McKeesport area. They knew one other, grew up together, and shared dreams together. That's another example of Herb's great, caring personality. During this time, his passion for race and equity was highlighted as he watched those he loved being treated with disrespect while they fought for their lives. Was it the disease that made others lose their compassion, humility, and care for human life? Everyone he knew who suffered from HIV was mistreated, but he witnessed a stark difference in compassion between black caregivers and white caregivers, who seemed to bring an added layer of fear and blame.

He and Chenits became close – finally a brother for Herb. As Herb matured, he remained committed to Margaret, who had a successful career in the prison system and law enforcement and retired in her fifties. They still struggle with their relationship sometimes, like many people. We often talk about what it really takes to make a relationship work – taking the time to get to know someone and love them for who they are, making a commitment to stay with them through the changes of life. We gave them some intense, fruitful counseling on communication and kindness while we were together in California for our forty-year vow renewal.

A few years ago, I experienced my only serious conflict with Herb. He and I had always talked about starting a business together, something sustainable for retirement. Chenits and I wanted to invest in a family enterprise that would grow. In addition to his soil scientist job, Herb was a driver for a tourism company in California, with local tours through the week and Las Vegas trips on weekends. Three or four years ago, he told us that a friend had lost his bus company. Herb was thinking about buying it and starting a bus tour business in Los Angeles. He asked whether we would be interested; Chenits and I were thrilled. We had several meetings about how to arrange the details – investments, percentages, and so forth – with them in Los Angeles and us in Pittsburgh. He even named the company P&L Tours – Pettigrew and Larkins. Chenits and I were going to invest eighty to one hundred thousand dollars. Herb had cashed in some of his

401(k) to buy the business and buses, but he kept putting off the paperwork for the partnership even though I had recommended several lawyers in Los Angeles who could provide the service.

Herb called one day and said he couldn't make pay-roll – he needed to borrow ten thousand dollars right away. We sent him the money without hesitation, but we wanted to know the status of our partnership and agreement. He gave us no clear answer – he would work on it and get back to us soon. The company seemed to be doing better when we got a call from Herb's wife, who was angry that he had given the former owner a significant percentage of the company – splitting it sixty-forty, with no percentage for the Pettigrews. I confronted him and demanded an explanation. He apologized and said the timing was never right to create a formal partnership. He offered to try bringing us in, but we were no longer interested.

I have found it in my heart to forgive him. He wouldn't agree to keep the money. Instead of a partnership, he offered to sign a promissory note; we declined. He sent back five thousand dollars and promised the rest soon. The business closed. Having such a major breach with Herb was very difficult for me. Chenits and I were the only family at his destination wedding in the Dominican Republic. Whenever he needed anything, we were there for him. He understands me more than my other siblings.

Herb stayed in California after his second divorce because he wanted to remain in his children's lives. He has been involved in all their ball games; all those things he wanted as a father, staying close and watching the kids grow up, especially his youngest son, Herb Junior.

Brian joined the military after high school and has stayed in for a decade. He married and had two beautiful children — more grandnieces and grandnephews for us to expand our precious legacy. He and his wife divorced; Brian found love again and fathered another child. Brian used the military to educate and discipline himself, as many have in my family — my father, my uncles, my father-in-law, my brother, my nephews, and more. Like many African-Americans, they put their lives on the line for the country that has not reciprocated with respect. Brian was in Iraq. He also learned a trade in the IT fiber optics space, and he is positioned for a successful career.

Herb Junior was diagnosed with juvenile diabetes in his early teens. Although he had several promising opportunities, he used his illness as an excuse for bad behavior, a great concern for our family and a trial for his parents. A few bad decisions resulted in a short stint in the prison system, a major disruption from which he had not recovered as the innovative, visionary young man we knew more than a decade ago. His parents loved him, coddled him, made exceptions, and gave passes. His father got him a job at the company where he is a soil scientist, but he lost it for unprofessional behavior — using company funds for personal business. His inattention to his health led to his getting a leg amputated when he was in his early twenties. He has survived two cardiac arrests. He has not been able to keep a job, he won't go to school, he stays home and smokes weed most days in spite his extended family's efforts to help him reach his full potential. He has lost his will to live. We're afraid we'll get that phone call one day, but my brother continues to wrap his heart and mind around this child. What made him take this path? Was the stress and expectation that as a black man he had to do more, be more? Was it the early bad decision that destroyed his self-esteem? Was it his illness? As a mother of three African-American men, I know too well how mall things can derail your dreams, steal your joy, and limit your opportunities.

Herb's first wife, Billie, married a white German man and had a daughter. Eddie, who remains married to Tina, developed MS but has become an ambassador for a German organization that promotes MS research. He has visited the United States several times to give personal testimony of his journey. Herb and Eddie have stayed very close. Herb has many positive, giving characteristics that still shape how I think of him as a brother, father, and friend. This is who he is in my life. He was the only sibling at the renewal of our vows in October 2018, and his musically talented friends were the hit of the reception.

Herb is slightly darker than I am but not as dark as Mary, which has always been a problem for her. We've always been concerned about where she thinks she fits because of her darkness in the family and wish she would let it go. Over the years, we have talked about Herb's experiences as an African-American man. He seems comfortable in his skin. He always teases my sister —she wears makeup that makes her appear lighter for pictures. People still use bleaching creams and other devices to lighten their skin. Many of us are still trying to assimilate by changing who we are, changing our skin color and hair texture. Very few beauty shops deal with styling of natural hair; thousands will help straighten hair chemically or otherwise. Straight hair is what gets you in the door most of the time as a black woman, but change is coming. An African-American man with locks has few chances for a good job without an extremely sought-after skill.

MARY ELIZABETH

Because she was the firstborn, conceived immediately after our parents married, Mary had to grow up fast – she spent much of her time watching us for Mom to make sure we stayed out of trouble, and she resented it. She was more tattletale than nurturer, but what more could anyone expect from a child left to raise her siblings? Her role was to let our mother know when we stepped out of line, not to help us grow or become better people.

My father was very dark, my mother very light, and Mary was the darkest of the children – a major drawback in African-American culture. She thought she received less love and nurturing because of her birth order and her complexion. She was denied a normal childhood, and she dated little. Her first boyfriend was also her first husband, Charles Martin Jr., known as Piggy. His family lived across the street from us.

One night when we were on the front porch, we heard a loud commotion from their house and Mr. Martin appeared in the middle of the street. My father joined him, they started arguing, a fistfight erupted that carried to the Martins' porch, and we joined the brawl that rose out of nowhere. Daddy later explained: Mary and Piggy had eloped some time ago without our knowledge, and the Martins had received a package meant for Mary. They had gone to Columbia, Maryland, where they didn't need a parent's signature despite their young age. She was pregnant. Another generation of kids having kids.

Mary was excited to leave our house, have her own home and family, and raise her son. They moved into one of the low-income housing units called the projects. When the baby came, they named him Darnell. Piggy was drafted in the military during the Vietnam War, when service all too often meant the young men might not come home.

When Piggy returned, Mary was soon pregnant again. Piggy clearly had undiagnosed post-traumatic stress disorder (PTSD). He was abusing drugs, especially alcohol. I watched heartbroken as Mary became a battered wife. Piggy, like many African-Americans with mental health issues, never got help. They lived in the projects in poverty, Piggy worked in the steel mill, and Mary took odd jobs to make ends meet. Many times she would call us to pick her up because he had beaten her so badly. My parents said, "When you've had enough, you'll leave. You can come home as much as you want. When you feel you can't take another beating and you don't want to continue a life with this guy anymore, you will leave and start caring for yourself." She went back and forth for years. Infidelity complicated the relationship. Mary learned that Piggy had fathered another child; she confronted him, which led to more beatings.

Finally, the breaking point came. Mary called Chenits and me to say she was taking the children to the hospital because Piggy had badly beaten all of them. The boys had welts all over their bottoms and backs, inflicted by their father. She risked losing them to Children and Youth Services. Piggy threatened to kill her if she left him, so we devised an elaborate rescue plan while she was staying with us. He wrote a letter saying, "I don't want anything, you can have everything, but I just want you, I want you to come home." Our strategy was for them to go on a mid-afternoon date, ostensibly to figure out how to reconcile, while my husband, his friends, and I would move stuff from her home to a place where she and the children would be safe.

I dropped Mary and Piggy off at a park with instructions to pick them up at an appointed time. At the move, I mostly gave directions. We left some things so Piggy would have a place to sleep and look after himself. When he returned home and discovered most of their things were gone, he started threatening calls – he even called the police to charge me with breaking and entering. Mary showed them the letter saying he didn't want anything, so I was not arrested.

Reflecting on my beatings from Momma and Mary's from Piggie made me ask: What happens when women get into such situations where they feel so powerless, so willing to do drastic things to protect their children? I thought about motherhood and mothering and what that meant for generations of my family.

Mary later met Frank, who became my brother-in-law. He was twenty years older and owned a barber shop with a beauty shop in the same building and, typically, gambling in the back room. She fell madly in love with him, and they were married for many, many years.

During that time, she changed in a way that disturbed me. I believed she was becoming more self-centered, abandoning our raising, our spirituality, and our sense of right and wrong. She entered a world alien to me, a world I thought was not the norm. Frank allowed gambling and sale of illicit goods out of the barbershop.

The barbershop was a hub of the African-American experience where you found out what was going on in the neighborhood – who died and who was born, who was more accomplished and who was going to jail. Here you made friends and heard gossip. You also engaged political debates, advocacy, Black Lives Matter, and hope for the community. Frank was a respected, socially active businessman, but, like everyone else, his focus was prosperity. The men who sold things in the shop were often addicted to drugs. They were trying to hustle and make a living in a place where few jobs were available to them because of their race, no matter how great their talent.

Mary had not graduated from high school, but she worked in the steel mill and got her GED. Sometimes she told me experiences with male coworkers who spoke coarsely and condescending about women, but she never suggested they disrespected her. She tolerated what I considered sexist remarks from white men about black men and women. After her GED, Mary earned her beautician's license and started working in Frank's shop. They enjoyed a full life traveling and raising her two children together. He had several children by his first wife, but only one or two came around; finally, only one stayed close to his father and welcomed Mary into his life. Frank and Mary were financially comfortable, so these kids were privileged African-American boys in a pretty rough neighborhood. Piggy was not active in Darnell's and Charles's lives until they were adults. He died in his 50s as a result of complications from alcoholism, but the boys stayed close to his family.

Mary was trying to parent on her own with our family's help. Chenits helped Charles get into college, but he dropped out after a year. Both of my beloved nephews sank deep into the drug business and the fast-paced money track with little thought of the damage to others' lives and our community. Both of them served and spent vast sums of Mary and Frank's savings in the judicial system. We often warned our children not to visit their cousins often, worried that they could be snared in police surveillance. I watched the so-called justice system work in my family and community – black men convicted for a first or second minor offense sent to jail for lengthy sentences. Our Caucasian friends and family members served fewer years for comparable infractions. We were living in *The New Jim Crow: Mass Incarceration in the Age of Colorblindness.* My family is among the statistics when author Michelle Alexander discusses the "racial caste" of the prison system that now controls the fate of more African-Americans than were enslaved in 1850.

Eventually, my nephews fell in love and had several children. I have many nieces and nephews from partners who were white, African-American, or West Indian. Mary has a host of grandchildren she absolutely adores, including Darnel's and Charles's children's children, Jarrell and Rhea Ann. She has devoted herself to protecting her sons as well as her grandchildren and great-grandchildren, leaving her and Frank in a difficult financial position. They constantly spent much of their savings, took out second and third mortgages on their home, and did all they could to cover attorneys' fees and bailed her sons out no matter what they had done.

Mary resisted accepting any woman her sons dated or married – none was good enough in her eyes. All mothers want their children to find mates who will love them, share triumphs, and care for their children through life's challenges. This girl was too fat, this one too skinny, this one too white. Concern for how an interracial couple could thrive in either the white or African-American community remains a challenge for most parents. Sometimes after she got to know the women, she grew comfortable, sometimes not. Race was always part of the conversation.

In many families, the maltreatment of our ancestors instills fear because it still happens from many who consider people of color as targets for disdain and disrespect. Some of the white women casually said "nigger" as part of their squabbles or slang. White men and women who have become a part of our legacy sometimes imagine they fully understand the black experience. Some grew up with such privilege they could say "nigger" in front of the descendants of slaves. Mary appreciated humility and compassion, but she disdained condescension and stereotypes of black women's relationships with white men. She was trying to protect her sons the best way she knew.

Mary was tired of raising grandchildren – a few of the women were good mothers who worked hard and took care of their children, but others left their upbringing to her. She was still shuttling kids to school and buying their clothes, still trapped in the motherhood role that started in her teens, making sacrifices while ignoring her own needs.

One white girlfriend became pregnant while using crack cocaine, went into premature labor, and delivered a baby boy tiny enough to hold in one hand. In a wee-hour conversation, Mary told me, "I'm not doing this again." I convinced her that this little mixed-race baby was still her grandchild, part of her legacy regardless of drama around his birth. This baby is part of our us. Legacy and care for our children runs deep among African-Americans. Before the late 1980s, I never saw many black babies in the child welfare system because their families could not care for them as a village. Around this time, I noticed that many black children were being adopted by white families. It would take another book to explore the challenges these families face, from hair care to preparing them to navigate a world where racism has a life of its own. One worthwhile study is *White Parents, Black Children: Experiencing Transracial Adoption*, by Darron T. Smith, Cardell K. Jacobson, and Brenda G. Juarez. When Mary went to see this baby, named Chazae, my godson, she fell in love, took him home, and adopted him with Frank.

Mary and Frank had a great life together. Frank was always full of life when I was around him, always wanting to entertain and be entertained, always wanting to have friends and family around. He loved to barbecue at home with friends. He constantly quoted quips I'd never heard – "It was so quiet in there you could hear a rat piss on cotton." He grew up in Charleston, South Carolina, a descendant of slaves, and considered himself a Geechee, Creole-speaking people also known as Gullah who lived in the South Carolina Lowcountry and Georgia. He cooked spicy food rich with herbs and spices, lots of rice, with a mastery of a pinch here and a pinch there and no need for a recipe – a skill based on his Southern upbringing. He also had a way with profanity He articulated his passion for politics, justice, and even religion with hilarity. He spoke to Mary in a way I thought disrespectful, but they loved their life together. He never, ever hit her – he only took care of her.

I worried about the lack of gentleness and respect in their marriage, but I was ashamed of my judgmental attitude. Maybe they couldn't build a solid foundation for growing old together because of the financial burden of the children, grandchildren, and great-grandchildren. When Frank fell ill with a diabetes-related condition Mary became his primary caregiver. Then I saw the unconditional love I had overlooked. After Frank died at age 72, she was devastated. She was young and beautiful but never dated again, devoting everything to care for her family. The children and grandchildren took shameless advantage of her, staying in her house without paying rent or utilities, asking her to make their car payments, draining her finances without contributing.

Grandparents raising grandchildren is the reality for many women and families across this country, black and white, rich and poor alike. To this day, Mary has never had chance simply to enjoy life. Both of her sons have been seriously ill. Darnell had several heart attacks. Charles had a stroke, and Mary became his at-home caregiver. Her children neither respect nor support her.

Momma once told me she thought Mary lacked respect for her as a mother. When my father passed, Mom moved into Mary and Frank's attic. She called me and related disrespectful ways Mary treated her, much as Mary's children treated her. Momma felt she couldn't stay there because of the financial and emotional drain, so she moved to California, close to Herb, Chenits, and me.

After the trauma of Mom's death, I decided Mary and I must repair our relationship. Mom always said, "If nothing else happens to me in life, what I wanted most in life was for my children was that they would be friends and they would genuinely care for one another." We have tried to spend more quality time together, to understand things that bring stress and joy to each other's lives. We have become good friends. She was there for me when Chenits had a heart attack. In the past, she might go years without calling; now, she'll pick up the phone any time. As she's aged, she's grown more pleasant. Now the concern is: will she ever have a life beyond caring for her grandchildren? Will she ever be able to say no to her children and walk away from the drama?

I consider how my siblings and I arrived where we are. We endured tough times. The others never went to college, much less got an advanced degree. Everyone made their own way through ups and downs and can be very proud of who they are. Mary suffered from racism through her life – she tells stories of many toxic encounters with white people and her observation that white immigrants disdained her – part of their process of becoming "American." She has a few white friends and acknowledges the ones who have recognized her talent, treated her kindly, and offered opportunities. She worked as a steelworker, a hairdresser, a medical clerk in a hospital, and a certified nursing assistant over the years – a career path with financial security and engagement with interesting people and ideas. She has a reflexive mistrust for white folks until they prove their sincerity, like many people who struggle with the colors of their heart.

FAITH ANNETTE

I was five years old when my sister Faith Annette was born, a premature delivery that consumed the family with hospitalizations because of her many physical problems. She was so tiny that my mother called her Peanut, a nickname that stuck for life. We siblings resented the demands on Mom's time. We'd tell her that she wasn't really our sister – she was found down by the river and our parents decided to raise her. We had to take care of her, and she would often tag along when we went to hang out with friends, but I have few memories of her younger years beyond the beatings and ridicule we both received from our mother. Faith was also a longtime bed wetter.

My clearest memories start when she was a senior in high school. It was a predominantly white school on the east side of Pittsburgh with more to offer than our old high school, but she felt singled out and slighted as a black teenager. She had few friends, suffered exclusion, and was barely passing with no mentors or sponsors to guide her. The only thing offered was slipshod service from the counseling staff. She wanted to become a nurse, but she married Butch right after high school, had a daughter, Nicole, when she was twenty, and had another daughter, April, when she was twenty-two. By then, Herb and I were living in California.

Faith got deeply involved in a Church of God congregation, a very conservative Pentecostal church – we called them Holy Rollers – that culturally and intellectually distanced her from the family. Meanwhile, she and Butch got into debt, and she showed little ability to keep house – when I visited, it was chaotic. Faith had a falling-out with the church and with family, so she asked to come to California for a fresh start. She and the girls would stay with Chenits and me at first, and when she got established, Butch would join them. We decided to support her.

Adding Faith and her young girls to our small house was a strain. We were living paycheck to paycheck, and she ignored our frugal routines of laundry (she washed several times a week) and meal preparation (she made breakfast of meals prepared for dinner). Her habits stretched our patience and our resources. I came home to find the house in disarray and the meals scheduled for the week already eaten. She and Butch separated for good.

Herb and I got Faith on public assistance, registered in college, and moved into a small apartment in Los Angeles so she could get on a career track and take care of her children. Within weeks, she met a guy named Wayne who quickly moved in with her. They drank heavily and experimented with drugs. The children told us they bathed with Wayne, a red flag although we had no proof of abuse. With my mother in Los Angeles, we confronted her with our concerns over lunch in public. I led the conversation. It did not go well. She accused me of trying to take her children from her because I had no daughters and always wanted a girl, then she stomped out of the restaurant. She rebuffed my efforts to reconcile and told me I was out of her life – she never wanted to see me again. Her boyfriend threatened to kill my whole family if I tried to contact them again. Chenits and I decided to back off for the good of our children. We didn't speak for several years. Momma, who had her own small apartment in Los Angeles, and Herb maintained contact.

Faith spiraled into crack cocaine addiction, and she and Wayne lived transiently from hotels to friends' houses. Butch divorced her, she married Wayne, and they moved to Oakland where they put the children in school and tried to establish themselves. We feared Faith had turned to prostitution, which she vehemently denied although she had seen other women choose that route.

Faith and the children once visited to Los Angeles at my mother's insistence, emaciated for lack of nourishment. Because Mom didn't drive, I sometimes took her to visit Faith. Only then could I see my nieces. Once she was living in deplorable conditions at a hotel where the children slept on a couch. She was bringing up her children as she had been brought up, with beatings and face slaps that sometimes left them crying for hours. But she wasn't raised in an environment of filth and disarray.

Nicole and her boyfriend Franklin were about thirteen when she got pregnant. She had lived sometimes with his family. When I took Mom to Oakland, we found Faith and April living with strangers in a house without so much as toilet paper and toothpaste. Nicole and her baby son had moved in with Franklin's generous and supportive family. Faith was angry that she had lost Nicole's welfare check that helped support her and April. "How do you end up thinking this way," I asked Momma. "How do you live in a society that's supposed to be so promising to everybody and end up in this space where you are depending on your children for your livelihood?" My family talked often about poverty, disparity, racism, and race. I later found those topics summarized well in "Welfare Money Is Payoff for a Lot of Things Besides Welfare," in the June 2019 edition of *The Atlantic*.

I was angry that Faith still consumed so much of my mother's time and robbed her of so much joy with her self-centered, manipulative approach. Public assistance was taking care of Faith's daughters and grandson, but that so-called safety net was not designed for her, and she continued to drain Mom's resources. Both of them suffered from her addiction and lack of access to treatment.

After Chenits and I moved back to Pittsburgh, Faith decided she needed to come home, get into rehab, and restart her life. She brought April with her, but Nicole stayed with her new husband's family, where they flourished. As April approached her eighteenth birthday, Faith worried about how she would survive without the government assistance that comes for her child. She was a welfare mother trapped in a system with no opportunity, self-respect, or motivation. She was mistreated by social workers who disdained her, and at the same time, she was gaming the system to survive. She leaned on her family, and we supported her for the sake of the children even though we knew it made her more dependent. Mom often asked us to pay her rent or other expenses, all the while begging us to become friends.

April, her beautiful younger daughter who had cognitive issues and took special education classes in high school, was suffering because she could not join after-school programs for lack of transportation and money. She could read at only a fifth-grade level, but she found a full-time job while in school to help the family. Then Faith went to school, became a nursing assistant, and landed a full-time job. She was excited about the opportunity to lift herself up, become a better parent active member of society. I set out to rebuild the family, spend more time together, organize vacations in California, and pick up the check for meals and special events.

Mom moved back to Pittsburgh and took out credit cards for family members who ran up debt with the expectation they would pay her back. Chenits and I vowed to protect her. We paid off all her bills and gave her one credit card that was supposed to eliminate the others. Since she didn't drive, she depended on Mary to run errands; and when Mary's car needed tires, she expected Mom to buy them. Mary doesn't remember this, but I can't forget how this abusive and disrespectful demand devastated Mom. Mom had come a long way from our childhood days of beatings – now she would do anything to please us. Faith paid inadequate attention to financial management because she expected family and friends to cover her. Once when she got a tax refund, she gave Mom fifty dollars. Mom was so proud and excited about the gift, but I was boiling inside: "Are you freaking kidding me? I have traveled with you all over the United States of America, bought groceries, paid bills." I felt my sacrifice meant less to her than fifty dollars. I yelled how disappointed I was for her to brag about this daughter who brought her nothing but pain. I should have directed my anger to my siblings for taking advantage of her – they were again using her credit card for themselves – but I took it out on Mom. I saw her joy disappear and instantly regretted my selfishness. I apologized, but it still hurts that in that moment, I robbed her of knowing she had become the mother she wanted to be, and Faith valued her. The experience made me a better mother, with a better measure for value in life.

On the day Momma died suddenly, Faith was out getting her hair done for an evening gala – using Mom's credit card. I had to settle Mom's estate, pay off debt, and make funeral arrangements. Meanwhile, some valuable pieces of jewelry disappeared from her house. Mary, Herb, and I pooled the cash sent with condolence cards, but Faith kept hers.

I struggled for years to honor Momma's wish for her children to be friends. I finally reached a point where I have forgiven Faith – not forget what happened, but understand her life and what she has gone through – a young women with the trials of women of color in this country, her faith, her dependence on others, her poor financial and relationship choices, her addiction. Her issues are not just personal irresponsibility or inadequate parenting but full context of rejection and despair. Elaine Richardson chronicled the same circumstances, and her path out of drugs and human trafficking, in *Poor Hoe on Dope to Ph.D.: How Education Saved My Life*. a despair that, from the outside, looks like a failure to care for their children or take responsibility for their life. She was lucky. So is Faith. Many women never escape.

In 2017, April had a baby, Brianna, giving Faith another chance practice positive mothering. She looks after that granddaughter most of the day. Brianna, a very happy little girl, is the center of her life and conversations. I pray Faith will never resort to her hands for discipline. I want to know and love her better. When I see the vast national response to the opioid crisis that affects so many suburban white people, I contrast the failure to respond to the heroin and crack cocaine crises among inner-city black people when Faith needed more than we could give, and there was no other support. Faith and I came from the same hardworking parents, the same family, and led such radically different lives. She still says she wants to be like me. I want all of society to learn what I have – to seek the best for everyone so we can all flourish. Only the whole society can heal the whole society. When the person can't, when the family can't, when the neighborhood or city can't, we must look to the larger community that can.

PART 11
LATER YEARS

COLLEGE

*If you are always trying to be normal, you will
never know how amazing you can be.*
~ MAYA ANGELOU

I was the first in my family to go to college. My mother
had completed eighth grade, my father high school.
Chenits put together a financial aid package for me and
educated my parents concerning the college experience.
My parents loaned me fifty dollars for books.

So I could go to college, my mother agreed that she
would keep Carlos during the week, but I would have to
come home every single weekend to take care of him
no matter what. In high school, I would have to come
home from school and wash diapers and stay up with
him and do all those things that were important to do
in order to be a good mom. I did that. I knew I could
do this too.

Roy would show up in Pittsburgh almost every
night and stay with me in the dorm. He would question
what I was doing, whether I was talking to other boys.
I thought he was very jealous. I now know this abuse
stemmed not from jealousy but from fear that he would
lose his power over me and that someone else would
love me. I soon discovered he had no love for me at

all. The abuse was about control and feeling superior to someone he didn't value. The beatings started again. He had been beating me before I had my baby, but the beatings became more intense later – punches in the face like he would hit another man. He would show up drunk, question why I was going to college, and start beating me no matter what I said. One night, I fought back. We were in a fistfight – I felt like I was fighting for my life. He had me on the floor with his hands around my throat, banging my head against the floor while screaming: "Don't you know how much I love you, bitch!"

I silently prayed, "Lord, if I ever survive this night, I will never take a beating again." That was the last time. I didn't see him as my boyfriend ever again. I locked my doors. That was it. He was no longer part of my life. I knew he didn't love me. I knew that wasn't love. I didn't want this in my life anymore. I wanted to succeed in college, and I had to expel him from my life to survive. Roy stayed in our lives because of our son, although I never asked for child support. I gave Carlos my last name. He was my son, but I allowed Roy to see him. He picked up Carlos one day to visit his mother in West Virginia. I was waiting for him to come back on Sunday night. I called frantically, leaving messages with his mother and sister when he didn't show up. When I finally reached him, he told me that Carlos was his son too and he would keep him as long as he wanted because he had rights. He asked me why I was bothering him. My prayer was that he would bring Carlos back to me. He did. After that, he didn't have him for ten years, so Carlos didn't really get to know his father until he was in high school and reconnected in an ongoing way. That child saved my life. I only hope Roy appreciates the value of this gift as well.

That's how I've lived ever since. My children have been the center of my universe; to this day, they are everything to me. They are my heroes because they could do all those things children should be able to do to become the best they can be. Because of Carlos, I wanted to live, and I wanted to be a good mom. That is what kept me going.

I could not escape the psychiatric challenges that threatened my definition of self. I was probably nineteen when I started therapy, after a failed suicide attempt that led to the help I needed. I felt that Carlos didn't really need me because my family surrounded him with so much love. He was the grandchild who really needed them. I was a student; I needed them as well. They gave him anything he wanted. The only beatings he got were from me – they gave him love and care. By this time, Chenits was in my life, and he loved Carlos. We started dating when Carlos was a year old. Before that, I was going home every weekend, trying to take care of my son but feeling useless and inadequate as a mother. That sense came from everyone in my family, especially my mom, who constantly reminded me that I was just not good enough. I began to believe she could love my child more than I did. She fed my insecurities. I'd put on a dress and she'd say, "That's a cute dress, but it would look better on me." Eventually I fell into a deep depression. I understand why people contemplate suicide. I was in this spiral of feeling worthless. I could not satisfy my mother. I could not satisfy my God.

I'm still very religious. I know God put me here for a specific purpose, but then I felt everyone would be better off without me on Earth. I loved my son, but other people could care for him better. I took an overdose of pills, had my stomach pumped, and started seeing a psychiatrist. The few sessions I intended made a big impact. The therapist said, "I'm not here to solve your problems. You have to figure this out for yourself." He believed in me. He said, "You have to dig very, very deep inside yourself, push beyond the pain because inside you will not find this quiet, 'everything's going to be all right' person." He showed me that I would never reach my full potential until I realized how important I was to myself and then to other people. Why should you think your life should end now? You're not supposed to choose when that happens. Was I strong enough to live this life and do the things I want to do? What stands out most of all from my sessions with him was my confusion around being a child of God and understanding that I was not God. The line from the popular rock opera "Jesus Christ Superstar" hit home: "Who do you think you are?" You're not the one who can solve everyone else's problems. You're not the bad person. You're not inadequate and unable to take care of your child. You are a child of God, and a person who should have purpose and live your life according to what he wants you to do. You need to find that purpose. You should work every single day to be the best you can be. "The best you can be" has become my standard advice.

I walked away from that psychiatrist with a brand-new perspective on who I was and who God was. I had a journey to take, rewarding and challenging, and I set out.

As I progressed through nursing school, I noticed that many of the women who had started the program with me were dropping out – a few the first years, more the second, more the third. Some went home, some changed majors. I never asked why. I didn't know them well. I was maintaining in the program, not a stellar student but writing my nursing care plans, going about my work, and completing my assignments. In the third year, a nursing instructor pulled me into her office and told me I had failed one of my clinical clerkships and probably couldn't finish the program because of my lack of writing skills. She had no complaints about my patient care or staff communications. It was all about my written care plans and my reflections. She went out of her way to say that she understood most black children who come from segregated or predominantly black schools have the same problem. But I didn't come from a predominantly black school, and she couldn't explain exactly what was wrong with my writing.

I showed my work to Chenits, who was still working as a minority recruiter for the university, and he saw nothing wrong. He contacted someone else and then suggested I meet with the Dean of the School of Nursing. After I explained the situation, they confronted the instructor, Ms. Conte, and I was allowed to continue, apparently on probation with close monitoring and critique. I realized this was probably why my classmates dropped out – they were up against subjective, biased critiques fed by living stereotypes. I was ashamed that I had been so distracted and detached, maybe too self-absorbed trying to survive myself. By the time I graduated in 1976, only two of the twenty-one women of color who started were left – and the other one was so light-skinned she could have passed. My grandmother's voice echoed: "The closer to white you look, the better your chance of surviving in this world." My day of excitement and pride was overcome with sadness. No one crossing that stage looked like me. The entire nursing school had only one African- American instructor, Mrs. Parker. I never took a course with her, but she was always very encouraging and reached out to see how I was doing.

This bias on the basis of color still distorts evaluations today. I see it with students in medical school. I think about this history of African-Americans in the country – the lighter you were, the more opportunities you had. Either you passed or you were close enough to get the nod and go on. People my shade or darker didn't have those opportunities. This prejudice infected the African-American community as well. My grandmother insisted we couldn't marry anyone of a darker persuasion. I considered her racist – but how could she be both racist and African-American? It was the mother in her, the grandmother in her, who wanted to protect us in a world that was so unforgiving when it comes to color – and still is.

I still experience ups and downs in my life, with a nagging sense that I wasn't the best I wanted to be, particularly not the best mom. Chenits had fallen in love with my son. He would provide for Carlos, but I wasn't sure he loved me. I felt a constant pull to claim what I believed belonged to me alone – this person I loved dearly, whom I birthed, whom I sought to ensure the best in life. I needed to have him away from my family and away from Chenits. I wanted to be the mother I longed to be.

After some turmoil, I left Pittsburgh, moved to Maryland, and got a job as a nurse in Washington, D.C. I felt I was getting on my feet at last. I had a child with me whom I could love and who loved me, and I could finally do all the things I wanted to do for him – the life I never had. Life was challenging living in D.C., but my family still supported my growth.

My Dearest Margaret,

I was once told by someone wiser than I that some of us get to choose the path we take. For others the path is chosen for them. For me you have been written into my destiny from the beginning. I was on the path to a love that has only grown stronger through the transition of our life together you have been lover, partner and friend. I came back home to say," I thank you for the forty plus years that have brought life, love, fatherhood and joy and a quest to become my best me.

My life has been greater than imagined because you were the path chosen for me. As our journey continues, I know we will walk hand in hand in the clutch of circumstances as one.

You are my love, you are my life.

Love always,
Chenits

CHENITS

Chenits Pettigrew was born in the Hill District of Pittsburgh in 1947, the only son of Chenits Pettigrew and Virginia Wheaton Pettigrew, the only child of Sarah Frazier and John Wheaton, the son of Barry Wheaton. Chenits Sr. is one of seven children born from the union of Lillian Ballou and Thomas Pettigrew. Both Sarah and John were born in Anderson, South Carolina. Sarah's mother was Sally Walker. Chenits' parents divorced when he was three, and he was raised by his mother with little contact with his father, who married again and had another son, Ronald. Chenits keenly felt the absence of his father and longed for his approval. Thomas never attended a football game when Chenits was playing through high school and college or attended any milestone celebration. Many African-American men – young, grown, and fathers themselves – suffer this void.

Chenits, by contrast, is a wonderful father to his sons. Such positive black male role models are vital for African-American children and youth who remain targets and victims of structural racism. Chenits remembers growing up in the Hill District of Pittsburgh, raised in poverty by a mother who struggled with that racism. Both lived in fear of making wrong choices, always alert for whatever could derail their hopes and dreams for a life of prosperity and security that never came. Chenits feared both whites and blacks as he sought to navigate his own neighborhood.

His mother worked at a laundry, then a restaurant, then in housekeeping services with Blue Cross and Blue Shield until her retirement. He learned to navigate inner-city Pittsburgh alone, going downtown to shop for shoes when he was just eight years old. The city was enjoying the jazz explosion with stars like Billy Epstein and Nancy Wilson. Chenits had many African-American teachers and classmates but few close friends and little sense of belonging. He often hurried home, varying his route to elude the bullies that sought to beat him up – just like many children today.

Chenits attended Westminster College in New Wilmington, Pennsylvania, a historic Presbyterian college where he still felt isolated, both in the rural white community and on campus, despite his role on the football team. He tells many stories of being a black man living in white America. His experiences became life lessons for our sons.

During George Wallace's campaign for president in 1963, Chenits offered a ride back to New Wilmington to a white female classmate on his debate team who was stranded after a match. A Wallace rally had just ended nearby. A group of white men noticed the black man with a white woman and chased Chenits after he dropped her off – he made it to campus fearing for his life. Later, he was arrested in Washington, D.C., for driving while black. A Jewish friend bailed him out.

Chenits knew the trauma of encounters with white police officers long before Black Lives Matter elevated the focus on those injustices and the daily toxic stress they inflict. He was violently arrested on the University of Pittsburgh campus when he returned to his car to get his briefcase and a white woman who assumed he was stealing the car called police. He scrupulously avoids calling attention to himself while driving, never even slightly breaking the speed limit, and he raised our sons with a laser focus on staying safe and knowing how to respond when accosted by white law enforcement – stay polite, keep your hands on the wheel, make no sudden moves, and obey. Only black parents must instill that life lesson, with fear as a motivating factor. Safety is the key to survival. Be aware of where you are, who you are with, and what you choose. That is the necessary, but not always sufficient, stance with people who make assumptions when they see your skin color. All the boys encountered this prejudice – stopped while driving while black, followed by security in department stores, receiving an undeserved low grade, suffering exclusion from peer events. They all watched less-qualified white men land jobs and win awards. Chenits taught grit, confidence, self-worth, legacy, and integrity. He taught the boys to give people who don't look like them a chance to win trust as friends and colleagues. He became the father he was looking for – present, available, and transparent.

I was sixteen years old, a sophomore at McKeesport High School, and a member of the Future Nurses of America when Chenits came to speak. I was considering a career in medicine despite the discouragement of my guidance counselor, and I volunteered as a candy striper at the local hospital in the summers. Chenits, a recruiter for the University of Pittsburgh, described a new program for African-American women where they could study in the summer and earn admission to the school of nursing with a grade of C or higher. I knew this was what I wanted to do. Admission to majority institutions, especially in nursing, historically excluded black women. Here was a chance.

Between that meeting and my matriculation into the school of nursing, Carlos was born. I met Chenits again during orientation and quickly fell in love with him, but we didn't date for a year. I lived in the freshman Towers dormitory then moved into the nursing dorm farther from most campus activities. Chenits always seemed sad when I saw him, and I tried to cheer him up. One day when I answered the phone in the dorm, I recognized Chenits' voice and told him I was Delarese, a student he had recruited. We chatted briefly. He was kind and genuinely interested in how I was navigating school. He asked to speak to someone named Rhonda who was visiting her sister. Turns out she was his wife and they were getting a divorce. I had seen this man when he was happy and when he was miserable.

Months later, I was parking my old green Ford on campus when he happened to pull up behind me in his Mercedes. We talked, he asked me out, I said no. I had to go home and take care of Carlos. He said he'd like to come by and meet Carlos. My having a child was not off-putting to him – he eventually loved Carlos before he loved me. That weekend, he came to my home, some distance from campus, and visited us. Our first official date was a boat ride on a Gateway Clipper cruise.

We dated throughout my college years. Sometimes he took me or both of us on recruiting trips all over Pennsylvania and Delaware. He was funny, smart, and a gentleman. We spent hours talking about life, history, politics, and the future of our county. We were both opinionated and adamant about our solutions to racism in America, hunger, and world peace. I was finishing nursing school and living with my parents when my friends reported whispers that Chenits had another girl living at his house in Pittsburgh. He always gave me his car when he was away, so one weekend, I drove to his house, knocked on the door, and told the woman who answered who I was. She recognized me as Carlos's mom and pleasantly invited me in to talk. I told her that I loved Chenits and we were together. She pointed out that she was living in his house: "He wakes up in the bed next to me every morning." My life collapsed. She saw his car when I was leaving and asked me to tell Carlos hello. That was the deepest cut of all: he had introduced my son to this hidden other woman.

I fled Pittsburgh, moved to Maryland, and got a job as a nurse in Washington, D.C. At last, I was getting on my feet. It was me and Carlos, we loved each other, and I could finally do for him all the things that were not done for me. A month later, I discovered I was pregnant with Chenits's child. Trembling, I called to tell him. He was quiet at first, then whispered: "You know what you have to do." A knife went through my heart. Surely he was as frightened as I was – bringing a child into this unstable relationship was overwhelming. I never expected such an assault on my self-worth. I didn't know what to do. Life was out of control again. I was alone. Confused and depressed, I decided to terminate the pregnancy despite my faith, a decision that still haunts me.

Like so many women of all races and ages, I faced the choice of abortion or raising another child alone. The procedure was psychologically harrowing. The physician reinforced my shame of the pregnancy and my unworthiness. I was alone through the process, and I wept the whole time in the quiet room. When it was all over, I asked whether the physician could tell whether it was a boy or girl. "What do you care?" he said. He only reinforced my confusion, guilt, and lack of self-worth.

I can relate to women who abort a child. I believed mine was in heaven by my own hands. Sometimes our decisions are outside right, wrong, or reason, but they are our decisions. I can't imagine my life if I had another child without a partner. I have devoted my life to help other women have that choice. Color is an extra limiting factor for many women who face hurdles of racism, access, poverty, and inadequate health care. As an abortion provider, I served many white women who excused their choice by imagining unique challenges. Many of them had protested with anti-abortion activists and would go back to challenging choice for others.

After the abortion, I fell into a severe depression, failed the nursing boards, and settled for a job as a nursing assistant at a much lower salary. I was barely surviving. I sent Carlos to live with my parents and cut off all communication with Chenits.

I met and married Jimmy, a street-smart guy just out of prison. It was a short courtship. He was so different from anyone else I had known. He was struggling too, but he treated me well. I needed kindness. I needed time to find myself and heal. We tried to make it together for Carlos, him as a janitor, me as a nursing assistant, living just below the poverty level. Our brief marriage gave me a chance to grow. Momma reported that Chenits survived a car accident – maybe a suicide attempt, but I doubted it. He remained close to my family after we separated, and he kept sending me notes before I married. He always asked Mom to tell me how sorry he was. He denied any relationship with the hidden women. I remember only the pain.

Living in D.C. with little support was tough. Momma insisted that I come home and let Chenits take care of me, but I kept mistreating myself. I numbed myself with weed. I didn't want Chenits in my life, only Carlos. I even stopped smoking to convince my mom I could care for Carlos, but Jimmy kept smoking and experimented with other drugs, including angel dust that made him mean and irritable. He didn't abuse me physically, but he made up for it with verbal abuse.

Then I discovered that he wasn't hitting me because he was hitting my son. I unexpectedly picked up Carlos from school one day, and he said, "Where's Daddy Jimmy?" I said, "He's not available, so I'm picking you up today." He seemed happy, so I said, "Why are you so happy?" Then Carlos told me that Jimmy would hit him, even for small things like not tying his shoes. What had I done? My son was being abused. This was my fault. I had to get him away from Jimmy. Life was out of control again. I called my parents for help to move out, and they sent money to get our own place. Jimmy found it and stole it. I called Mamma again, and she sent another envelope. Later, I learned the money came from Chenits.

I moved into a two-bedroom apartment that I assumed was less habitable than Cabrini Green in Chicago, so roach-infested that Carlos rushed to finish his food fearing the roaches would get to it first. I passed my boards and landed a job as a nurse, but I was still spiraling downward. I was failing as a mom and sinking deeper into depression.

Chenits called one day – the sound of his voice still wounded me, but he asked to visit us, and I agreed. When he came, we took a long walk and watched Carlos play, a happy little boy without a care in the world. "I want to take care of you and Carlos," Chenits said. "I love you, and I love Carlos." I doubted anyone loved me because I didn't love myself. I thanked him and said I would think about it. When he asked whether he could buy some things for us, I said I didn't need anything. "I'll just pick up a few things," he said.

A package arrived a few days later – a brand-new nursing uniform. I realized how dingy and tattered my old one was. I was a single mother in poverty. I called Chenits and asked, "What does it mean that you want to take care of us?" He said Carlos and I could live with him. He reassured me that he would be the person I had fallen in love with. We moved home to Pittsburgh. Chenits traveled with Carlos and sometimes my mom traveled with them. Carlos thrived. I forgave Chenits for the pain.

I worked in Pittsburgh for a while, but Chenits' family did not accept me – they thought I was a threat to the successful life he had built. We decided to leave Pittsburgh so we could grow as a couple and establish our family. We moved to Los Angeles where my brother was an artist. That far from my family, I soon saw myself differently – smart enough to earn graduate degrees, to be a good mother.

LOVE, LIFE, AND LOSS

The sorrow we feel when we lose a loved one is
the price we pay to have had them in our lives.
~ ROB LIANO

In 1978, Chenits and I had married, I was pregnant, and we were building a life in California. I was working at the Veterans Administration hospital in Los Angeles when a premonition swept over me so horrible that I vomited. Soon, I got the call that my father had died from a massive heart attack. He had just recovered from a heart attack a year earlier, but his follow-up care was inadequate — no diagnostic or preventive interventions. Like many African-American men, he was not offered the most advanced treatments routinely available to white men — not even a baby aspirin. He was stricken on a ladder while painting the ceiling. He was fifty-two. I was twenty-five. I had lost my idol, the one who never spoke a harsh word to me, who was so joyful and encouraging.

Daddy was celebrated in traditional African-American style followed by a military salute that brought tears to my eyes. After we buried Daddy, I realized that Mom had reverted to a fifteen-year-old. He had catered to her every desire, even driving in the middle of the night to buy what she craved. They were a beautiful couple – I remember them dancing in each other's arms – but she never had to grow up. She couldn't write a check, pay bills, or even drive. She had been utterly dependent on him. Now she was overwhelmed at the prospect of losing their house and making her way alone.

Who would fix the roof? Who was going to manage the finances? Who would love her?

Mom sold the house, moved in with Mary, and started her independence, her voice. She turned to Chenits and me constantly seeking advice – and confiding the struggle of life with Mary, who she felt failed to show her love and respect. She finally moved to a little home near us in Los Angeles to start rebuilding her life – socializing and keeping up with her children and grandchildren. I saw her transform into an absolutely wonderful, active, caring person. We became close through her frequent travels with Chenits and me and her help with our children. With wisdom and humility, she taught me to bathe, dress, and nurture our babies – to become a great mother and wife. She became my best friend. We held hands like two schoolgirls when we shopped, and we lovingly signed cards and letters with YBG (your best girl) and YOM (your only mom).

Mom had a happy life in Los Angeles, despite her concerns for Faith's family. She visited the Dollar Store every day and fell in love with Gary, a young man she met there who loved her, cared for her and took her to wonderful places. She spent most of her time with him and talked about him constantly. One day, she called me to get her to his house quickly – Gary had called complaining of severe back pain. I called 911 as soon I arrived, but before the emergency workers arrived, he died in her arms. She was so distraught that she never dated again, instead devoting the rest of her life to her children and grandchildren.

Chenits and I were committed to having dinner as a family, talking about current issues, and studying with our children. Momma had a big role. My children remember her only as they wonderful person she became. Partnering with Mom, we brought up our sons to understand that they were going to encounter racism. We said it's like the weather: when it rains, it may come as mist, a light off-and-on drizzle, or an overwhelming monsoon. Sometimes they need to put up their umbrellas – guard their hearts and head out of the storm. Sometimes they should stand; sometimes they should back away. They could die over little things. Being black in America imposes unimaginable stress, but my children have established great relationships with white people because they have great hearts.

MOMMA

The mistreatment of Momma by her nieces and nephews started as soon as she returned to Pittsburgh. Family members took advantage of her desire to care for her grandchildren, her lack of skills at budgeting, and her generous heart. I tried to protect her. Momma often traveled with us and attended beautiful formal dinners and galas. She and I enjoyed running errands, going to movies, and spending hours talking. Some evenings we'd empty a couple of bottles of Champagne while we mused on life. She taught me what mothers should teach their children. She saved my marriage but never meddled. She showed me I was worthy and told me she was proud of me. The pain and sorrow of our past faded, and her voice still reassures me.

I was not always kind to her. When Mom's close cousin in Michigan died, Mary and I took her to the funeral. Mom packed for me, but she forgot my pantyhose and I exploded when I couldn't find them as we dressed for the ceremony: "Why can't you just do what I ask you to do? Now my outfit's not complete!" Mary, always on the lookout for a wedge with Momma, retorted: "How dare you talk to our mother like that?" My response was out of line and hurt my mother. I thought, "How complicated is motherhood?" Our relationship endured, but I regret that moment to this day.

On Friday evening, October 20, 2006, Chenits was being honored by the University of Pittsburgh with the prestigious Sankofa lifetime service award, especially his work to boost enrollment of underrepresented minorities like me. The award, with an African image of a bird facing backwards, honors those who give back, reach back, and bring forward those less fortunate.

A frantic call came from my sister Mary: "Mom is dead!" Those words still haunt me. Momma had been dressing for the gala when I called her earlier. She had fallen down the steps and broken her neck. Herb, who was picking up his tuxedo for the evening, discovered her body blocking the door when he went to the house. The coroner arrived before I did. Momma was gone.

Her death changed my life. After months of prayer, writing letters to her, going through stages of sad, angry, happy, exhausted, heavy with grief, I leaned on the words of a good friend: I was a good daughter. "You loved one another," she said, "and I would see you often walk hand in hand, laughing together and crying together." Momma taught me that black women must never walk with their heads down or feel less-than. We are a power to be reckoned with; love has no boundaries; our black brothers, who bear the brunt of our challenges in America, need us always to have their back. Humility is strength, and those who lack it will have a weaker legacy. She had only an eighth-grade education, but this beautiful light-skinned woman lived a full life and earned the respect of many.

CAREER IN MEDICINE

Chenits worked at Cal State Northridge and UCLA, then went to Tuskegee, Alabama, where he became a leading scholar in civil rights, human rights, and diversity and inclusion. He devoted his life to making sure that children of color had access to higher education. He was Vice President of Enrollment Management on track to become a president of a historically black college or university. I watched him navigate academia while keeping his focus on black children who need history, life lessons, and the chance to become their best selves in a not-so-kind white world. He offered the same caring and gentle spirit to every student entrusted to him. Chenits grew tremendously both as an academic administrator and as a black man who could embrace his passion and purpose to improve the lives of others in the struggle. He gave that up to support my dream of going to medical school.

I had seen the disparities in treatments and outcomes between whites and people of color ever since I started volunteering at McKeesport Hospital when I was in high school. I saw that white people were most able to walk the halls while people of color were sicker and more likely to stay bedridden. I realized that in the medical field I could improve lines with equity as well as health. I joined the Future Nurses of America despite my counselor's urging to focus on homemaking – my home economics courses and my incompetence at a job in a store's fabric department proved that wasn't my thing.

I got into the nursing program at the University of Pittsburgh, graduated despite some teachers' bias, and finally became a nurse. I had great mentors, beginning with Chenits, then a group of pioneering African-American doctors, Morris Turner, Robert Thompson, and Robert Kisner, who owned the only black obstetrician/gynecologist practice in Pittsburgh and served women far into the countryside.

I worked in medical-surgical nursing for a while but spent most of my career as a critical care nurse, looking after the sickest patients and their anxious families. I saw racism and sexism impact physicians' care as well as patients' attitudes. There were so few black nurses that even African-Americans distrusted me, assuming a white nurse would give better care. I often went home heartbroken. Some whites were openly hostile – one young accident victim spat on me whenever I approached his bedside. I had to focus on the good in people, whoever they were, to keep practicing in such a high-risk, toxic environment.

I became a nursing instructor and leader in critical care where my behind-the-scenes access gave me doubts about many medical professionals' character. When bed space was limited, older people were moved out of ICU for younger, women for men, and people of color for whites. The people of color would get sicker and re-admit more often. Transplants were available for white people who needed them; people of color almost never got them except from family members. That still happens. It drove me to focus much of my career on diversity and inclusion.

It also drove me to become a doctor. When I tried to understand my patients and their illnesses so I could be a better nurse, doctors told me that wasn't my business – those things were on a need-to-know basis, and I didn't need to know, even though I was at their bedside 24/7.

I also faced my own shortcomings. I was caring for a young anorexic woman whose family was sacrificing to help her. I couldn't understand how she could starve herself like this, but I related to her relatives with empathy and professionalism. One day at the nurses' station, when the others joked about her weight loss, I had joined the laughter when I turned around and saw her father. He had heard. I was devastated. I didn't challenge my coworkers. I didn't defend his daughter as a human being with a family who loved her. He never mentioned it to me, and I continued to serve them, but I worried that I had lost their trust. I decided to devote myself to becoming a servant-leader.

I had worked as a critical care nurse in a VA hospital in Los Angeles when we started seeing immunosuppression patients who turned out to have AIDS, before HIV had been identified. These were typically servicemen who had sex with other servicemen when that could get them a dishonorable discharge. The staff treated them with great fear and disrespect. Their suffering reminded me of slavery. They were dying around me. My faith called me to act; I often left churches that preached AIDS was God's punishment for sin. I wanted to uphold dignity and respect, diversity and inclusion, and I needed a stronger voice. I asked a physician once about electrolyte imbalances in a young man dying of renal failure, and he said: "You don't need to know that. You're a nurse. That's a doctor's job. He's going to die anyway."

I went home and told Chenits I needed to go to medical school. He said, "Go now – you're not getting any younger." We were living in California, raising three children, living from paycheck-to-paycheck. My nursing school GPA was 2.9. We were going to need help.

I became a nurse practitioner taking care of adult women and got a master's degree in education, boosting my GPA to about 3.8. By then, we were at Tuskegee and Chenits was on track to become a university president. I was accepted to medical school at Morehouse, close to Tuskegee, but when I asked to defer because my family was in transition, they refused. I was also accepted at my alma mater, the University of Pittsburgh. "We will wait for you," they said. "We need you. The world needs you." That encouragement confirmed this was my path. This coal miner's daughter had found her purpose. I was going home.

We still needed money. An African-American veteran, Colonel Mazyck, helped me apply for a military scholarship and get commissioned. This was my ticket to medical school. I took an oath that I would die for my country. I had opportunities to resist bias in the military, where mistreatment of women, gay, and transgender people was rampant – a microcosm of society.

I was alone in Pittsburgh with some support from Chenits' mother who had opposed our marriage and my sister who didn't understand medical school life. My mother had moved to Tuskegee to help Chenits with the children. I struggled with the separation: Is this God's purpose for me? I am a mother who really wants to be home when my children come home from school, to bake cookies, to read stories. I was away from my husband, falling in and out of depression, having palpitations, not taking care of myself, torn by the dilemma.

Many people at the university, black and white, rallied around me. Sandra Murray, the only tenured African-American professor in the medical school's basic science courses, faithfully supported all the minority students. Dr. Robert Connamacher, a white pharmacist, tenured professor, and passionate social justice advocate, taught me that I must call out the lack of equity in health care: Everyone is more vulnerable if the vulnerable lack care. Blacks who succeed must reach back. Meanwhile, I was getting double-edged reviews from white professors – "you're OK for a black girl" – and overt racism elsewhere. A prominent professor told me a promising woman needed me to mentor her because "she always walks around like an angry black woman." I never felt I belonged. I'm still subject to bouts of imposter syndrome that especially afflicts people of color.

I was working at Magee Women's Hospital in Pittsburgh and joined the African-American obstetrician/gynecology practice whose doctors mentored me while I was in nursing school. They agreed that I could go back after a year and pursue a career in infectious disease such as HIV and malaria, but when the time came, they reneged. I was the only black female obstetrician/gyne-cologist in western Pennsylvania, and I had a six-month waiting list. After about six years, I did a fellowship in HIV on my own time, earned a master's in public policy and international affairs, and started working in Swaziland with HIV-positive patients, especially women. I was teaching at the medical school and mentoring and sponsoring students.

After I became a physician, I renewed my passion for HIV patients, including those overseas. I joined Global Links in Pittsburgh that provided equipment to caregivers in Latin America and Africa; I later became the agency's chair and president. I served on the board of the YWCA, assisting women who had been evicted, and in the Action Against Rape organization.

In the early 1990s, I worked in Budapest -- where handwashing was invented in 1846 -- because obstetrician/gynecologists were not washing between deliveries and women were dying. The midwives were functioning as nurses; as a nurse who had become a physician, I could identify with them. I helped them change the culture, incorporating handwashing and wearing gloves. While I was learning about maternity wards, Chenits toured the country's history and architecture and developed a passion for travel. We have observed the differences in health equity in countries with varying degrees of development from Europe to India – a separation of the haves and have-nots, usually people of color. Why is such bias built into our everyday lives?

In Budapest, I saw a health care system that had no significant role for women because physicians were in charge – and physicians were all men. I never met a female physician, and I never met a male nurse. Even the nurses who cared for women did not respect women, and the male physicians did not care for the women until time for delivery. The situation is not much better in the United States. Nurses are on the front line of medical care, and in obstetrics and gynecology, where time is of the essence, their eyes, ears, and expertise are vital to prevent mother and child deaths. I faced bias as an African-American woman in particular. Not many people in the Romanian medical field look like me. I came home determined to make international promotion of better, more empathetic care for women and minorities a cornerstone of my career.

In the late 1990s, I went to Ghana with Project Africa Global, a nonprofit that offers medical tourism as well as educational program for students, faculty, and others from all disciplines. Condessa, my sister in faith, had agreed to become medical director for the group, but she received duty papers as an Army officer and needed someone to take her place. I volunteered, unaware of the challenges and rewards awaiting.

The trip was planned by a man who leveraged it as a way to spread the gospel while delivering medical care. That concept intrigued me – more than ninety percent of Ghanaians identify as Christian. I later realized I do not belong in an organization ties religious conversion to basic human necessities – a common strategy in poor countries. I was an obstetrician/gynecologist and wanted only to bring wellness to needy women and families. My group consisted of some 20 people who seemed to be roleplaying Tarzan. White or black, we had come to bring hope, save lives, and save souls. The journey wound up saving my life and giving me unexpected purpose and direction.

We rose in the morning after a restless night in fear of large rodents in our sleeping quarters. After early morning devotions and breakfast, we went to the Buduburam refugee camp to dispense medications, give dental and medical care, deliver babies, and distribute the Bible to presumed lost souls. The camp, about three hours from Accra, the capital, housed more than 33,000 refugees who had fled from the brutal Charles Taylor regime in Liberia. There, I met incredibly courageous women, men, and children. Some had been born and raised in this camp, and I was assisting in the birth of their children. Those children would sustain their parents' hope for repatriation to a homeland without war or another country where they could find better life. Our long days were filled with grace, mercy, endurance, and an inexplicable love of life amid such poverty and loss.

In addition to poor Liberians, the camp held members from royal families who had left behind their wealth but not their sense of entitlement. They established a class system amid the turmoil where there was little safety or security. Many of my patients were rape and abuse victims – displaced persons paying the cost of war. I saw acute, chronic, and communicable diseases not seen in the United States. I saw the fear of living without immunizations, readily available antibiotics, simple life-saving respiratory care, restorative therapy, or dental care beyond pulling teeth to prevent sepsis and death. Mental health was not treated and not considered a medical condition. Moderate depression was viewed as a major character flaw addressed only with guilt that imposed a sense of inadequacy and incompetence. Lithium, the common prescription for treatment, exacerbated the downward spiral with dangerous side effects.

In Kumasi, Ghana's second largest city, I employed all my skills. I helped the only skilled obstetrician/gynecologist perform hysterectomies, diagnose reproductive cancers, and discuss infertility as a national crisis. Women who could not conceive faced rejection and divorce. This drove my quest to grasp the significance of legacy, tradition, family, and the African proverb "it takes a village." I learned from every encounter with patients, doctors, drivers, dressmakers, and restaurant owners, but my greatest lessons came from my American colleagues. I saw their genuine desire to serve these needy people, but they lacked cultural humility and acted with unexamined prejudice. My own behavior revealed the pervasive reality of both unconscious and explicit bias.

In the late 1980s, the king of Swaziland asked my global health team to come help improve the care of mothers and babies who were dying in the early years of the AIDS epidemic without testing centers or treatments. They found an affordable antiretroviral medication in China, and I saw how Big Pharma's profits impact health inequity. I was teaching physicians and traditional healers how to care for HIV-positive obstetrics and gynecology patients through their pregnancy and after delivery. The culture views women as reproductive vehicles and controls them with shame and guilt. If a wife is not pregnant within two years, her husband can divorce her; if he dies – as many did in the epidemic – and she doesn't marry his brother, their land reverts to his family and she is banished. People in Swaziland are living longer now than they were when I started the work, thanks to medication and international aid as well as a decline in HIV infection rates.

We left Swaziland, worked in Malawi, then went to India to study the effects of HIV, mostly among sex workers who didn't use condoms and had to return to work after treatment in order to feed their children. There is no equality without equity. We are all missing what brilliant minds in Indian slums and U.S. inner cities could offer because they lack opportunities to contribute.

In Haiti, we saw how farmland abuse led to famine and how the ecosystem affects health care. We cannot solve the problems of global health without addressing every component.

My most recent international healthcare experience was in Guyana, notorious for the Jim Jones cult where more than 900 followers died after drinking cyanide laced Flavor Aid in the jungle. I worked with the government and others on a comprehensive plan to change culture and behavior, not merely provide medication and education. That included a program to train obstetrician/gynecologists as specialists taking care of women. After a decade, deaths of mothers in childbirth and stillbirths have dropped by half. We can do that in the United States. Why do black babies die at a rate three times that of white babies? Why do more people of color die from cardiovascular disease, cancer, and so many other illnesses? Racism impacts both access and decision-making both here and in Guyana. When Chenits conducted an orientation of physicians of Indian, Portuguese, and African descent, he noticed that darker-skinned ones are never respected or in charge. This discrimination prevents our flourishing as a healthy society.

People overseas rarely see African-Americans, especially women, volunteering in such situations because most blacks are busy taking care of problems in the United States. All the men and some of the women objected to my leading strategy discussions. One young man loudly asked, "Who is that Negro over there giving orders?" When I went fuming back to the hotel and told Chenits, he said, "Well, Honey, you are a Negro." He was referring to the historic reference to all Africans in American slavery at a time.

I asked my practice to decrease my time to eighty percent clinical, twenty percent academic research focused on global health and developing programs for women locally and abroad who were losing babies, especially HIV-positive women. They refused because they didn't want to lose the income from my longstanding patients. They attempted to damage my reputation at the university and in the community, where they were revered. I left and went to a Catholic hospital where I couldn't talk about birth control, much less abortion – and I had been an abortion provider. I am pro-choice and cannot grasp the lack of empathy, judgmental attitudes, racial disparities, and discrimination woven into this controversial procedure. White women rationalize their own private abortions while demonizing women of color who make that difficult at great personal cost in order to care for their families.

I had lectured in Cleveland for several years when a friend asked me to start a global health program bridging local and international communities. I went to work at University Hospitals and Cleveland Medical Center, the only African-American at my level was an assistant dean in the school of medicine working with students – I replaced the previous one who had been there for seventeen years. I was drawn by the mission to serve the underserved in the community.

Like many U.S. institutions, University Hospitals Cleveland Medical Center has added diversity and inclusion to its core values, but its long habit of white male leadership and the legacy of unconscious bias hinders its care in a community that is more than half African-American. The women in the organization who sought to advance their careers often accepted mistreatment and condescension to become perceived as team players.

Navigating such a system takes tremendous grit. Many people are not always honest, transparent, or concerned about integrity. I have suffered exclusion and disrespect from both blacks and whites whose daily decisions are life-and-death for many people. Empathetic people of color in the organization's lower ranks often gave up research careers to serve sick people on the front lines, but they have no power over policy – meaning inadequate care for poor white patients as well as minorities. Some leaders are learning more about equity and inclusion. I hope a philosophical and intentional commitment to address racism and the social determinants of health remains a primary objective.

How did we come to the place in our society where people are disenfranchised in the justice system, in education, in transportation, and other central features of life as well as medicine? Your ZIP code predicts your life span; your last name closes some employment doors; your speech hinders your self-improvement. I wake up every day thinking about being black in America. I'm in the C-suite where some people are surprised I'm articulate, where some branded my passion as "angry black woman" (no one was an "angry white woman"), where kindness and good intentions evaporate when you challenge someone who doesn't look like you, where greater talent is no guarantee of advancement but white skin is. We see this in every professional field, but it is a life-or-death threat when a provider's blind spots prevent effective care. Bias kills patients. Bias kills careers. Bias kills relationships. Bias stunts growth. People are denied opportunities because of some perceived misstep, where "tolerance" is a cover for lack of acceptance and inclusion. How did we get to this place in society? My recent visit to Gettysburg, Pennsylvania reminded me of three fundamental issue that costs 720,000 soldiers their lives during the Civil War; the survival of the union, the fate of slavery and common rights of citizenship that should be available for all Americans. The Union was restored and for a short time American honored our constitution that all men are created equal. America quickly forgot the humanity, equality and relinquish white supremacy was part of the definition of citizenship.

Douglas A. Blackmon's book, "Slavery by Another Name: The Re-enslavement of Black Americans from the Civil War to World War 11, helps us understand that slavery in the minds of many never ended. Policies and legalized racist only begin to answer this question. We must commit ourselves to heal people and help them become their best selves. We will fail to see great change in our society until academia and healthcare commit to improve the lives of everyone. That won't happen until they see the many colors of our hearts.

The COVID-19 pandemic of 2020 reveals the effect. A government committed to protecting white privilege rather than common good in policymaking is responsible for the outsized U.S. death toll. People in high positions rejected medical expertise and failed to institute practices to protect everyone, with disproportionate death rates among black, brown, poor, young, and old people. The pandemic proved that the health of everyone depends on the health of the most vulnerable, and it could lead to greater health equity in our nation.

I have begun working with young physician-scientists at Case Western Reserve University School of Medicine, where I am an associate professor, assistant dean, and director of clinical excellence and diversity. Academia, like business, medicine, and other fields, still takes an inadequate approach to inclusion and has not yet overcome conscious and unconscious bias in evaluations, hiring and promotion, and personal and professional relationships. For me and others who look like me and sometimes suffer from the imposter syndrome in this setting, the road is long to the goal of inclusion and excellence for everyone.

First Year Cleveland, a citywide institutional collaborative program where I am a committee chair focused on dismantling structural racism, is a beacon of light in our community. Its mission is to reduce the death rate of black babies before their first birthday. Black women are nearly four times more likely than white women to have a baby born between sixteen and twenty-two weeks' gestation, according to analysis of six years of Ohio births published in the *American Journal of Obstetrics and Gynecology*. No one knows why. Longstanding daily and intergenerational stress likely contributes. The agency targets such major factors as racial disparities, extreme prematurity, and sleep-related infant deaths. It is working to dismantle structural racism, including housing, transportation, and food, in order to ensure equitable healthcare outcomes. I lived through many of those factors as a child. Now I can challenge the injustice.

I Hope You Dance
BY MARK D. SANDERS & TIA SILLERS

I hope you never lose your sense of wonder
You get your fill to eat but always keep that
hunger

May you never take one single breath for granted
God forbid love ever leave you empty handed

I hope you still feel small when you stand beside
the ocean
Whenever one door closes I hope one more opens

Promise me that you'll give faith a fighting chance
And when you get the choice to sit it out or dance

I hope you dance
I hope you dance

I hope you never fear those mountains in the
distance
Never settle for the path of least resistance

Livin' might mean takin' chances, but they're
worth takin'
Lovin' might be a mistake, but it's worth makin'

Don't let some Hellbent heart leave you bitter
When you come close to sellin' out, reconsider

Give the heavens above more than just a passing
glance
And when you get the choice to sit it out or dance

I hope you dance
I hope you dance

OUR BLACK SONS

The two white ambulance drivers saw a fortysomething African-American man with slightly elevated blood pressure who couldn't move his legs or get off his air mattress on the floor of a home still in disarray from a year-ago fire. They told him to take better care of himself. They told his frantic wife that if he didn't feel better, she should take him to the hospital. Then they left.

I knew immediately when my son's wife Connie called that morning to way that he had suffered a stroke – and every minute without treatment lowered his chances for recovery. Connie and a neighbor got him to the car and the hospital, where his stroke was diagnosed. No thanks to those ambulance drivers, he made a full recovery within a year. Was it bias? Was it racism? Was it incompetence? These episodes of maltreatment plague the lives of men and women of color.

My professional life is dedicated to fighting systemic racism, particularly in the medical field where bias can bring death. My own life since my first child was born has been a daily struggle to protect and empower African-American sons in society – while navigating my own blackness. Results are mixed. "I Hope You Dance" goes unfulfilled for many black boys.

Carlos, born in 1971, was followed by Chenits Reese Pettigrew in 1979 and Gaetan Lorenz Pettigrew in 1981. Bringing them up has been both the greatest challenge and the greatest accomplishment in my life. Every day, I have worried about their growth, their talents, and their very survival. Every parent wants the best for their children – opportunities to have full and flourishing lives. But Africans living in America face a unique fear of losing their sons – losing them at the end of a gun, a knife, or a police billy club; losing them to an educational system that fails to equip them; losing them to friends who lure them into dangerous circumstances; losing them to financial predators who coerce unjust rents and prices. We are "Africans living in America" seeking our roots so we can find a place to stand. Black is black in America because your origins were erased in the slave trade. Whites identify as Irish-American or French-American or German-American or Polish-American or Italian-American, not European-American; blacks are merely African-American. Racism still impacts people who look like me. Roberto Clemente, from Jamaica, repeatedly shouted that he was not African-American while he was unjustly arrested. Skin color is the issue.

Chenits and I celebrated every sign our approach was working – their independent thinking, their concern for others, and their capacity for dialogue about politics and communities and environments. We were pouring ourselves into them so they could be the best they could be.

CARLOS

Carlos's birth father, Roy, was my high school sweetheart. Turns out I wasn't his. My culture considered me promiscuous scum that would never amount to anything. The attacks on my self-worth failed – because of Carlos. He saved my life. Thanks to him, I found direction, focus, audacious hope, and the courage to transcend the myth of worthless black children having children. Children turn out to be great at forgiving and giving unconditional love. I was nourishing him, and he was nourishing me. If either of us was going to thrive, we had to do it together – trust one another, support one another emotionally, physically, and spiritually. He was the joy of my life. He wasn't planned – like most teenagers, I gave little thought to the consequences of my actions – but he is an unsurpassed blessing.

My parents also found joy in Carlos and showered him with gifts and treats. They supported me with tough love that enabled me to finish school and go to college but demanded I fulfill my responsibilities as a mother with the rest of my time – no nights out or weekend parties. I had to study hard, wash diapers, mix formula, and make sure Carlos was safe. I was responsible for two people.

Not long after Carlos was born, Chenits came into our lives. He was attracted to me, but I know he was also intrigued by this toddler's bright mind and relentless curiosity. Maybe he saw a bit of himself – the only son of a mother raising him alone. The first toy he brought was a stuffed Curious George that became Carlos's constant companion. I watched Chenits play with him for hours and work hard to understand this child as fully as he could. Chenits was Carlos's on-the-scene daddy.

Chenits and I had frank talks about racism with Carlos and all our children from a young age, when they were already hearing racist remarks and seeing racist behaviors. We wanted both to surround him with people who loved him and to warn him that others would treat him badly because of his color. I wanted him to think about his math, his science, his friends, his future – not constantly about his race. I wanted him to have the necessary double consciousness, to be able to handle confrontation with non-threatening tact to avoid physical or emotional attacks. I wanted him to hold up his hands when stopped by the police, to obey the rules, to stay within his color during dangerous situations, to stay alive.

But there were too many people around him who believed the stereotypes of ignorance and inferiority. I couldn't protect him from the fear he felt when stopped driving while black. I couldn't protect him from the low grades assigned by teachers with biased standards. I couldn't protect him from the fake-friendly white peers. He lived in a world of temptation, and he played its games. He started selling drugs in middle school as a pawn for older boys who didn't value his life or theirs. Why was it so easy for this child and many others to be tempted? We were middle-class black folks. We lived in spaces where this shouldn't happen. Our kids should be safe. This was a hard lesson.

Temptation came from both blacks and whites, but Carlos wouldn't recover unless we removed him from this space. We left those environments every time we discovered them, seeking safety. Carlos attended twelve schools before he graduated. He was in high school when Chenits became Vice President of Enrollment

Management at Tuskegee University, and he abused his new status. He played his music too loudly on campus; he appealed to his father's job when he was stopped for running a stop sign; he ignored his studies. When his friends were going off to college, he couldn't because of his low grades. He had met Rosa Parks, Louis Farrakhan, Dick Gregory, Desmond Tutu, and other luminaries, but he was still trying to find himself.

We sent Carlos to Alabama State in Montgomery where he could redo his senior year and earn his way into Tuskegee. This historic black college offered the hope and affirmation Carlos needed. HBCUs are essential for the growth of many young black boys – enlightenment, fundamental skills, and cultivation from folks who might not always look like him but always cared for him. Dismissing stereotypes and embracing legacy were part of the education. That was a turning point – he applied himself for a year, transferred successfully, and went on to get a Bachelor of Arts in political science. He later completed a master's degree in teaching with a teaching certification from the University of Pittsburgh and now teaches English. Carlos is a great teacher, going above and beyond to help his students attain success. He and his wife Connie nurture their kids to be their best.

At Tuskegee, Carlos fell head-over-heels in love with classmate Consuelo despite the evidence of her mental illness – he once called us for money to get another pair of shoes because Connie got angry and cut up his new ones. She was possessive and suspicious, calling to check up on him at all hours. But he loved her, we loved him, and we were willing to back his choices. His brothers objected to the relationship and her narcissistic behavior at our gatherings, not to mention the profanity in front of their grandmother and the violence – he never hit her, but she hit him.

Awareness of mental illness in America has come a long way in my lifetime, but stigmas and stereotypes persist in many communities, including among African-Americans. As with physical illness, African-Americans are often ignored, underserved, and treated as less-than by the professionals responsible to care for their mental health. My family has experienced the ravages of mental illness, including my own experience where a psychiatrist helped me escape the cycle years ago. Ever since Connie came into Carlos's life, we have coped with her illness's impact on our whole family, especially their three children. Her story includes vivid episodes of failure by both medical and psychological professionals, with disaster averted only when family intervened. It provides a window into what countless African-Americans, especially women, suffer even from African- American providers in a society where overt racism has ebbed but unconscious biases based on skin color and socioeconomic status still threatens wellbeing and lives.

Connie and Carlos have been together except for brief periods since college. From the time she entered our family, she brought turmoil, distraction, and insecure attention-demanding that suggested she had grown up at the spoiled center of her family. She lacked any sense of manners and boundary-setting. When Carlos and Connie announced they were getting married, Chenits and I had a heart-to-heart with them over dinner, laying out our concerns but promising our support.

I got a vivid insight into Connie – and into race in America – in 1999, when her master's thesis was failed and her professor refused to graduate her. He was right. Connie had written a superficial paper arguing that racism no longer exists in the United States. This was her experience as a very light-skinned woman who apparently grew up in a very white environment in Pleasant Hills, New Jersey. Our family conversations on race were foreign to her. Her perspective colored my light-skinned grandchildren's views – her older daughter once insisted she is caramel, not black, and her youngest claims to be not only Caucasian but also Canadian, a far-fetched failure to grasp what it means to be black in the United States. I explained to the professor that she really believes what she wrote. He insisted, for academic integrity, that she write on a more scholarly subject. She earned the degree.

The birth of Corbin, Connie and Carlos's first child, our first granddaughter, was a milestone for the whole family. The delivery was traumatic – an example of careless treatment of an African-American woman even though her doctor was an African-American man. Connie went into labor at thirty-four or thirty-five weeks and was diagnosed with pre-eclampsia. Carlos was alone with her in Maryland and staying in touch on the phone, where the baby's heart rate was suffering dips called deceleration that signaled danger. The doctor was not there. When Carlos told us that Connie's blood pressure was high, I called the hospital, identified myself as Dr. Pettigrew, and was connected to the physician's home phone, awakening him in the middle of the night. At first, he treated me like an uninformed in-law and assured me she was fine, but I insisted that the pre-eclampsia was worrisome because she's having decelerations. "My daughter-in-law and my son trust you, so I'm going to trust you," I said. "This is my family, my grandbaby. I'm going to trust that you're going to take care of them." When I called Carlos twenty minutes later, the doctor had arrived.

Very soon, we could see that this little girl, the family's delight, was suffering physical and psychological abuse from her mother, who used fear to control the child. I saw Connie hit Corbin violently only a few times, but Corbin told of other kicks and punches. She became a belligerent, moody person, but she has not been diagnosed psychologically. Sometimes she is insecure and doubts she is loved, but overall, Corbin is an outgoing, sociable young lady who enjoys cheerleading. She is now sixteen years old and wants to become a physician.

Connie's second daughter, Chase, was born without complications, and Corbin adjusted quickly to her little sister. But Chase, too, grew up in fear and doubt about her mother's love because of the verbal and physical abuse. She became a whining little girl despite Carlos's efforts to protect her. Today Chase is an intense thinker. She enjoys acting, singing, and dancing.

Connie then had a boy, Carson, in a different public hospital who assumed she was a Medicaid patient and treated her as less-than although he and Carlos were both school district workers with second jobs, good insurance, and a private provider. Although the information was on her chart, workers asked, "What clinic did you go to?" "Are you seeing one of the midwives?" No one called the physician of record because midwives typically delivered women from the clinic.

When I called the hospital room after Carson was born, the nurse told me that Connie was in the bathroom bleeding heavily. The white nurse had called the African-American female physician, but she had not arrived. When I called back, Connie said she was bleeding through her pads, then the nurse said she believed Connie needed a dilation and curettage, a method to remove retained clots or retained placenta – she had called the doctor several times. Again, I called the hospital as Dr. Pettigrew and got through to the doctor, who was irritated and dismissed the nurse's opinion: "I will make the decision whether anybody needs a D&C." I frankly replied, "I'm an obstetrician/gynecologist. I'm on my way. Based on what they're telling me, she needs to go to the operating room immediately. If anything happens to my daughter-in-law, you will be held responsible."

I hung up as she stammered, waited five minutes, and called Connie's room. The nurse answered and told me they were heading into surgery. Her hemoglobin was 5 – dangerously low, even after delivery, when normal is 12 to 14. She was bleeding and required a transfusion. If I had not intervened, she could have become another statistic on the long list of lost mothers I have spent my professional career trying to save. What happens to women who don't have a medical professional as an advocate? Have black professional started to also fail black patients by embracing the practice of classism that their white colleagues feel so comfortable with?

Carson is growing up a delight. He's smart, personable, and inquisitive. He reads and loves sports. He is both spoiled and suffering from his mother's wrath. He mostly stays away from the drama and finds peace in his electronics and television in his room. His mother still struggles with the effects of bias in this country and the mental illness inadequately managed for years.

I knew Connie had bipolar disorder before she was diagnosed, along with other issues like being histrionic. I could tell by her detachment from the family dynamic and her relentless demand for attention. For example, the entire family is diehard Pittsburgh Steelers fans; even though Connie professes to be a Jets fan, she went out of her way to root for the Steelers' opponent when we had friends over to watch a game. She seemed compelled to stand totally apart from who we were – her preferences in food, her refusal to swim or wear dresses – perhaps because she was trying to figure out who she was with an opposite stance that damaged our camaraderie and social relationships.

Connie can be pleasant in superficial public situations, unlike inside the home, but she has no sense of boundaries. Once at a comedy club where she roamed the room while the rest of us sat, I noticed her talking to a man at the bar who had his hands around her waist and touched her inappropriately. Rather than call attention, I just got up and said it was time for us to leave.

As a mother-in-law and medical professional who faced my own mental illness, I have tried to help Connie get a diagnosis and medication, which helps when she uses it. Carlos will not give up the relationship despite its damage to his own life and future. They moved away from us to Maryland, and their problems escalated – accusing one another of affairs, fighting in front of friends. Carlos, being co-dependent, tolerated her behavior until it affected the children.

One Saturday several years ago, Corbin texted me a picture when we were on the way to Washington, D.C, to see Corbin and Chase at a cheerleading competition, but I didn't open it. When we arrived, I saw a terrible bruise across Chase's face that was partly obscured by makeup. She explained that Connie was beating her with the belt on Thursday when she accidentally hit her face with the buckle; the coach tried to cover it up for the competition.

When I got home, I confronted Connie over the phone and said I was arranging her admission to a psychiatric hospital because of how she treated the children. Chenits drove to Washington, and Chenits Reese flew in from New York to help. They took her to the hospital, where she was evaluated for ninety minutes and released with an outpatient therapy appointment for the next week. When I heard that, I insisted they take her back and told the hospital as a physician that she was abusing her children, in crisis, and in need of psychiatric help. They admitted her. I am sure that she will never forgive me, but my hope is that she realizes that love drove that decision.

Nothing that extreme has happened again. How do I protect my grandchildren? So many people are falling through the cracks in society. We talk about how to be a good mother in family meetings, but Connie cares for the children for her own comfort zone, never taking them to swimming pools or the movies. She tells them she works a second job on weekends to avoid them. Chase, who asked us to send her to boarding school, said at a Christmas family meeting that no one, including her mother, loves her. All of us are trying to keep her well and save our family.

We cannot solve the problem of inadequate medical and sociological care for minorities in America by depending on minority providers. For one thing, there will never be an exact proportion of minority providers for minority patients. More importantly, the assumption that people who look like me will understand my legacy and culture and treat me better than others is not always true. I have seen it time and again in interactions with physicians of color, including women.

The solution is not the color of their skin but the colors of their heart. Vulnerable populations, no matter who they are, will suffer if their provider doesn't have a compassionate, humble heart that recognizes dignity and respect as paramount for excellence. Every caregiver must check their biases and commit to compassionate care for every person. They hold these individuals' lives – and their families' lives – in their hands. They must overcome blinds spots in their decision-making. If you don't see colors, all colors, and they're not part of your heart, you're going to leave people out, in medicine and psychology as well as in housing, politics, education, and every other field.

When Connie is drinking or not taking her meds, their house is in chaos. Carlos can't see the root of the problem, much less its solution. In November 2015, as we prepared to attend Gaetano's wedding in California, Carlos's house burned down while Carlos and Connie were at parent-teacher meetings. In his rush to get home, Carlos hit a curb, rolled his car three times, emerged safely, and ran home. The children were safe, but their home and all possessions were destroyed. We insisted they go to California for the wedding, a reprieve from the overwhelming circumstances, then they sorted out rebuilding with their insurance company. They made poor decisions on rehabbing and contractor selection and wasted insurance money on local con artists who promised significant savings that never happened. They lived with a friend for almost a year and were just back in their house when Connie called 911 and the ambulance workers decided the black man with high blood pressure didn't need a ride to the hospital. He recovered from his stroke.

Today, as they age and their children grow, they spend more family time and seem to enjoy one another. Connie is a hard-working school counselor determined to get her students every opportunity for success. She works to manage her depression, to stay motivated, optimistic, and sociable. We enjoy our grandchildren, who are born entertainers, and keeping us laughing.

CHENITS REESE

We were living in Los Angeles when Chenits Reese was born in 1979, the year after my father died. We made sure to tell stories about Dad so he would be part of his grandson's life. Now I see so much of my father's spirit in Chenits Reese. His measured and rational analysis of every situation is a reflection of Dad, along with his openness to share every part of himself with a positive attitude, always seeing the glass half full. My mother spent significant time with Chenits Reese, as with Carlos, nurturing him and having a big impact on who he is today. He was always very bright, inquisitive, and rational. He walked early, talked early, and showed a preternatural capacity for problem solving. He became an avid reader and philosophical thinker.

Chenits Reese attended costly Montgomery Academy when we lived in Tuskegee, our attempt to shelter him from the lingering overt racism in the South. All the children met visiting international African-American leaders such as Rosa Parks, Louis Farrakhan, Dick Gregory, and Desmond Tutu. Chenits became an early advocate of civil rights and human rights. Even in the South, but we were surrounded by people who sought to be more accepting and understanding of the African-American experience, even supporting real integration and reconciliation. But at his school he experienced, unconscious bias and racism, from his teachers. The children addressed their white teachers formally – Mr., Mrs., Miss – but called the food service and custodial workers, who were African-American, by their first names. When I pointed this out, the administration quickly implemented a policy of formal respect for all adults. I celebrated this small victory as a portent of bigger changes coming. The children became historians with phenomenal moments of inspiration they shared at the dinner table. We drove close to eighty miles a day to get them to this school that offered the best path to success, where they could focus on English, math, and science instead of the hostile treatment elsewhere. Then medical school and career changes took us back to Pennsylvania.

When we returned to Pittsburgh, we bought a home in North Hills so we could send the children to an excellent public school – investing in real estate rather than private education. We heard the area would be safe, but we faced housing discrimination. The owners of the first house we tried to buy reneged at the last minute; the Realtor told us they weren't willing to sell to an African-American family, so we found another. Pittsburgh had started a community-wide conversation about race, including the tacit redlining in many neighborhoods. The local newspaper featured our experience.

Although we were in the neighborhood, we did not fit in at the school. At my first PTA meeting, parents complained about the homework load and turned hostile when I supported the rigorous approach. My children, who had thrived in a demanding private curriculum, were told they had not scored high enough to join the school's gifted program. I was never allowed to see the scores, and I suspect someone made a biased decision. Worst of all, Chenits Reese was called a "nigger" by his classmate and responded with a vigorous verbal exchange that escalated to a fistfight. Rather than address the cause, the administrators chastised Chenits Reese and told me to call the other child's parents. They took the position that all "niggers" were violent; I excoriated them for their ignorance and told them I pitied children who grew up in such a home.

This is the experience of countless African-American children in the public school system. They are reflexively blamed for any problems. They are labeled ADHD or, worse, they become fodder for teachers' breakroom gossip. They face disproportionate threats of suspension and expulsion. We watched children suspended from kindergarten. Who suspends a child from kindergarten? Normal childhood activities among children of color are labeled behavioral problems, a slander that follows them through life. It happened to our children from a two-parent, middle-class family, and to the children of our friends. How much more does it happen to the children of poor single mothers?

We decided our children would not be physically, mentally, or emotionally safe in those schools, so we sent them to Sewickley Academy, a small K-12 school that was actively recruiting underrepresented minorities to boost its diversity. Sewickley upheld strict behavior rules and expectations. While the children sometimes felt excluded – there were only two African-Americans in Chenits Reese's class of eighty – they were safe, and they participated in sports and trips with the others. In that environment, Chenits Reese flourished as a leader and scholar.

As he went into high school, however, Chenits Reese wanted to play football in the upper division, which meant transferring to North Hills High School. We reluctantly supported the move. The school had become more tolerant. He enjoyed the high-level sport – one teammate went on to play for the Washington Redskins – and remained a top student in addition to a great skier, German speaker, and inquisitive traveler. When he experienced racist behavior, he talked to us, but supportive friends of diverse races and ethnic backgrounds surrounded him.

We belonged to Jack and Jill of America, a venerable organization of successful mothers raising African-American children that offered opportunities not always available in the larger society while sustaining connections to their legacy. Our family was an outlier in the aristocratic group with quasi-British activities like cotillion – we were more likely to have dinner conversation about driving while black and facing mistreatment in fast-food restaurants. But the club gave our children a safe and positive place to learn social skills, enrich appreciation for the arts, and develop friendships. Chenits Reese met his first high school romance at the club.

At the North Hills graduation in 1997, Chenits Reese received honor after honor for his community work, serving the poor and homeless, as well as his academics. He won a full academic scholarship to Penn State University, where he flourished as a student and worked in the black studies department and the Black Student Association. The group lobbied against discrimination, a lack of diverse faculty, and other issues so much that it received threats from people on campus and beyond. Because the students were ignored, they organized a sit-in on the football field before a Penn State game, where they were handcuffed, escorted away, and thrown into jail.

When that happened, Chenits and I, fearing the worst, drove all night to reach our son. I got leave from my military responsibilities. We knew nothing about how long they would be held, and they had no representation. Chenits Reese was released and not charged, but the story became national news. The Black Panthers came in, and the FBI investigated the hate mail threats, including one that referenced a young African-American man found dead not far from campus. Many students begged them to back down, but others organized major sit-ins in the student union. They attracted allies from other races and ethnic groups as well as LGBT students who insisted that people be heard. Chenits Reese walked across the stage at graduation wearing a bullet-proof vest under his gown because of death threats.

Chenits Reese came home to Pittsburgh and started working to make a difference in the lives of young children. He had launched a career in music and theater when he was fifteen and majored in communications at Penn State, so he applied those talents to help at-risk youth. He and his father were once interviewed by Tavis

Smiley's magazine about their experience at predominantly white colleges twenty years apart. They concluded that little had changed.

In Pittsburgh, Chenits Reese fell in love with a young woman who became like one of our children. She worked in a hair salon, decided to go back to school, and eventually earned a bachelor's in nursing. Together, they marched, protested, and advocated for people less fortunate, promoting the great things we have in common that can transcend division. In 2005, Chenits Reese moved to New York to get a graduate degree in business music management at New York University. The long-distance relationship was not sustainable.

All my sons are forgiving, welcoming gentlemen, mature beyond most of their peers, and emotionally vulnerable. Chenits Reese had been in this relationship for ten years, but they could never get to the point of committing long-term to mutually support and respect one another. When they broke up, he fell into a spiral of dark immobility that stifled his creativity. The healing came when he leveraged his music, his writing, and his poetry to look deeper into himself and see the contributions he could make as a productive and creative individual. He started traveling for the State Department under Hillary Clinton's leadership in a Lincoln Center program with Winton Marsalis that recruited talented young artists as ambassadors abroad. Hillary mentioned him by name in a national television interview. He visited war-torn countries such as Libya and Syria to teach children how poetry could help heal them. They created CDs and performances to deal with their trauma. The healing came when he used his music, his writing, and his poetry to look deeper into himself and see the contributions he could make as a productive and creative individual. He started traveling with Jazz at Lincoln Center on the Rhythm Road, a program started by Winton Marsalis sponsored by the State Department. They recruited talented young artists as ambassadors to other nations. As Secretary of State, Hillary Clinton was a proponent of the program. She mentioned Chenits by name when she was interviewed on national television. He went to Morocco, Tunisia, Algeria, Lebanon, Jordan, and Syria to teach and explore the universality of Hip Hop music and culture. He taught workshops, master classes and performed across the region that helped young people hone their voice and speak their truth.

Chenits Reese insisted that everyone – all racial and ethnic groups in the United States and abroad – must learn real world history to avoid making the mistakes of the past. In 2013, under his professional name, Chen Lo, he created Soundtrack 63, a live performance and multimedia presentation about the African-American experience in the United States. The show includes a strong dose of family legacy alongside historical events from before the Civil Rights Movement to the present. The event toured many cities and sold out the Apollo Theater in February 2018. His creative company Soul Science lab has since signed with Columbia Artists.

Chenits Reese found himself, his voice, and his passion. He also found Naana Badu, a first generation Ghanan-American who descends from the Ashante tribe. Chenits and I knew from our DNA test that many of our ancestors came from Ghana. We had visited there and explored two slave dungeons, caverns underneath a Roman Catholic Church where captive Africans were held before shipment to the New World between the sixteenth and nineteenth centuries. This slave trade, also known as the African Holocaust, arrived in the United State more than four hundred years ago. Central and West Africans were sold by other Africans to European slave trader – first Portuguese, then British, French, and Dutch – a total of more than 12 million robbed from their homes. Illegal smuggling continues today. On our visit, we reached a door that read "Door of No Return" on the inside, but "Welcome Home" on the outside. Ghana, like Liberia, was a welcoming West African nation for descendants of U.S. slaves who sought to return in the nineteenth century.

I met Naana on a layover in New York when I was flying to Guyana and she was visiting from Los Angeles. She worked in management consulting for Deloitte and planned to move to New York to start her own fashion business. Chenits Reese was entertaining her for a few days, covering for a mutual friend who had been called away. They were both graduates of Penn State where they had known each other but never really connected.

As soon as I saw them at the airport, I knew they had a great chemistry for friendship, but marriage didn't cross my mind. Chenits Reese had recovered from a devastating relationship and reclaimed his usual creative, innovative self. He and this accomplished, poised, gracious, inspiring woman could enjoy a powerful mutually supportive uplifting relationship. I delighted when they began to date. Soon after, when Naana lost her brother, I saw deep empathy for her in Chenits Reese. Then when Chenits, his father had a heart attack and Naana came to support Chenits Reese, I saw the same empathy in her. She is his soulmate, and she is a blessing to everyone she touches.

Some native Africans often draw a sharp contrast with African-Americans who carry the legacy of slavery and Jim Crow – and many consider themselves superior. They resent being treated like African-Americans by white people, especially police officers, in the United States. Rather than solidarity, some insist they should not suffer the same treatment as those people who just happen to look like them. All of us are Africans living in America.

Chenits Reese underwent cultural vetting from Naana's family. They wanted to be sure he was worthy of Naana's hand and was a partner who could strengthen and continue their legacy. Once, another of Naana's brothers visited us and we half-joked that he was evaluating whether we were worthy.

Both our families maintained the tradition that a young man asks a young woman's father for her hand in marriage. Naana and her parents came to visit us to talk about legacy and honor and integrity. Around my dining room table, Chenits Reese announced that he had already asked for Naana's hand, then her father spoke about the history of the tribe and their devotion to family, country, and legacy. He had evaluated Chenits Reese and found him worthy for his daughter, so they would welcome him. Her mother agreed, Naana said she had chosen the marriage, and her father pronounced his blessing on the joining of the young people and the families. Chenits talked about his joy that Chenits Reese found someone to love for the rest of his life. He gave his blessing.

When my turn came, I said we could not know whether we descended from kings and queens in Africa because our ancestors were stolen, but I knew we came from proud people because of our hearts. I recounted the legacy of being brought to this country against our own will while believing in God's will that we were chosen to live here amid the challenges and build our own legacy as strong people. We were proud that Naana had chosen Chenits Reese and agreed to join our legacy to hers. A sacred silence filled the moment: two powerful legacies were uniting. The wedding in May 2017 was a two-day event representing three distinct cultures – modern African American traditions, Ghanaian traditions, and that sign of resistance from the days of slavery: jumping the broom.

GAETAN LORENZ

My youngest son was given two Creole names from Chenits' Louisiana family — Gaetan Lorenz. He was a quiet, introverted child who never considered being sent to his room a punishment — he always found plenty to read or do when misbehavior exiled him from our family time. Gaetan was creative at making up stories and more — when we visited a friend's house with all-white carpet, he saw a blank canvas for drawing with a colorful marker. This artistic bent later found expression in paintings and charcoal drawings, even pottery. We were still an economically struggling family, and we were laser-focused on bringing up these three African-American men well. Gaetan suffered the typical taunts, teasing, and scapegoating as the younger brother, but he managed it by reaching quietly within himself. We had to train him to be sociable — before family events, we would practice how to step forward, offer his hand, and answer questions.

We were living in Tuskegee when he was in elementary school and sent him to Montgomery Academy. He eagerly recounted the day's events when I picked him up, until one pivotal afternoon. He had been crying uncontrollably, traumatized because a teacher believed a classmate who claimed Gaetan pushed him (another kid did the pushing) and called him a liar when he refused to be sorry for something he didn't do. She isolated him in another room, pounded her fist on the table, told him he was bad and always would be, and berated him until he apologized to end the torture. He was still weeping when he told me about it, and my heart broke for this little boy – my little black boy. I believed, but could not prove, that race was a factor – the teacher and accusing child were both white. My son would probably be subjected to this type of attack on his self-worth through life. Black parents must constantly protect their children from such people.

Gaetan was timid for years until he started playing sports – lacrosse, soccer, swimming, skiing – and shone. By then, he was at Sewickley Academy where he was surrounded by whites and attending a church where he was surrounded by African-Americans. He couldn't escape the racist rants of fellow players' parents, color-tinged jokes at his expense from classmates, or detention by police for driving while black. He grew more sociable while remaining serious about his academics, and he excelled.

Gaetan was accepted to Penn State while Chenits Reese was there. He attended for one semester before his brother called me to pick him up because he was in trouble. Gaetan seemed depressed, and we brought him home, wondering whether the transition from the small private school to the huge state school was too great a shock.

Finally, Gaetan told me: He is gay. His coming-out at school was interpreted as misbehavior. My response was: OK, you're gay; let's talk about it. I had been around gay people all my life as a physician, and I wanted to help him, not judge. I had suspected for years. When he came out, he was ill prepared. A friend called and begged him not to believe anything his parents said because we didn't really accept him – I saw the peer pressure and lack of support this population suffers.

A private talk with his father did not go well. I knew Chenits grew up in a culture that instilled homophobia. Once, in a restaurant owned by a gay friend of mine, Chenits told me to guard his drink when he went to the restroom because he was afraid of what could happen in a gay bar. Another time, he called me this "everything is going to be all right and God loves everybody" person, and I said, "If you believe in God, how can you be so bigoted?"

When Gaetan came out, Chenits told him neither God nor Pettigrews respected homosexuality. This uncharacteristic response disrupted our home; however, rejecting Gaetan was not an option. To love him was to accept who he was as a gay man. To know God is to love everyone. My pastor once taught on "God so loved the world" with heavy emphasis on "world." Not part of the world, not the heterosexual world, not the white or black world, not the Jewish or Muslim world. The whole world. All of us. So why do religious folks ignore "world" and justify bigotry? "Values," "ethics," and "legacy" cannot mask prejudice. Chenits and I both needed to grow. I came to understand the experience of gay men, especially African-Americans, in America, as well as what it means to be such a man's mother. Chenits faced a steeper learning curve to overcome his childhood teachings, but he persevered. Defense of bias comes from fear or learned ignorance. Gaetan's brothers, by contract, accepted his identity immediately and loved him unconditionally. Gaetan was their shy, loyal younger brother who was smart, funny, and part of us.

Gaetan found himself while we found our better selves. He stayed with us in Florida, took classes that transferred to Penn State, and studied dance at the community college for fun. The teacher told him he had career-level raw talent; he was teaching and doing choreography by the end of the semester. When he announced that he wanted to explore dance, I objected, but Chenits took him to the School of Dance in Miami for an evaluation. The teacher confirmed his raw talent as well as the market for male dancers and his career potential. He transferred to the University of North Carolina at Greensboro, where he began to explore self, date, and enjoy a normal college life.

One day, Gaetan called to say he and some friends were going to Washington, D.C., to audition for the Alvin Ailey American Dance Theater. I tepidly encouraged him – don't be disappointed if you don't make it, failing won't make you a failure, give it your best shot. He was accepted for the summer, then invited to stay in New York for a year as a fellow. We couldn't afford it, but a gay couple in New York, Kenny and Otis, our good friends agreed to sponsor him. When he was invited for another year, I said he should first go back to Greensboro and finish his degree first, which he did.

When he came home to Florida, he got calls from friends about an opening at the Bill T. Jones Dance Company. He got the job and toured the world – Chenits and I saw him dance in Paris. One day, he ran into Eartha Kitt in line at Starbucks. They talked about dance and life and career, and she told him dance was a selfish career – always focused on staying fit and toned and ready to be on view – that could end any time through illness or accident. A year later, Gaetan quit dancing and was taking courses at Columbia University to get into medical school. I saw mature independence and focused direction, but I was sorry he was leaving his delightful self-expression in dance. Gaetan wound up at the University of Pittsburgh Medical School, where Chenits was an assistant dean and their bond grew. He first lived on campus, then moved home.

Gaetan fell in love with a young man who might have become a long-term relationship, and he was crushed when the man was unfaithful. Love and pain are no different between same-sex couples as opposite-sex couples. Still, Gaetan grew into an outspoken observer of world issues and advocate for gay rights. He encountered bias at medical school that taught him to practice double consciousness, which he perfected during residency.

In his last year of medical school, Gaetan met Chris, a blond, blue-eyed white man from a North Dakota family of hunters and gun enthusiasts, and fell in love. From the beginning, we knew Chris was different from the others, who wanted Gaetan to change and didn't want to join our family. Chris was struggling with his identity and had not come out to his parents. They were dating when Gaetan started residency in obstetrics and gynecology, a last-minute switch from transplant surgery. Within a year, they were engaged. This was a new legacy: a white man was going to be our son's husband. We had not contemplated this in our lifetime of fighting for racial justice. Chenits grew up perceiving white men as the enemy. We had to grow again.

Gaetan embraced residency in Cleveland while Chris was in California, setting up a long-distance romance that provided little opportunity for the rest of the family to get to know Chris. When they got engaged, we scheduled more contact so Chris could understand the African legacy and activist mission of our family, from Kwanzaa celebrations to civil rights advocacy. We held a festive holiday gathering in Cleveland where the young couple's love bonded our vastly different families. Their wedding in California in 2016 was a spectacular event, with friends and family from all over the world at a night-before event in Pomona and a ceremony in Pasadena. It was the first time a Pettigrew married a Caucasian, let alone a member of the same sex. We sustain open, frank discussions about race, we hold remote monthly family meetings, and Chris is working hard to learn the culture of his new, black family and overcome his own unconscious bias. Gaetan is still learning about himself and his challenges as a black gay man in a white-dominated profession. They are both practicing physicians. Chris conducts research that takes him to Uganda and the Philippines; Gaetan specializes in transgender surgery and has received funding to launch a transgender surgical service in California. Both are committed to caring for populations that have been marginalized and disenfranchised. They are a proud part of our legacy.

PERSONAL REFLECTIONS

*At the end of the day, at the end of the week, at
the end of my life, I want to be able to say that
I contributed more than I criticized.*
~ BENÉ BROWN

The process of setting down my own story has involved reliving memories – all kinds – and seeing the events of the past with a longer view and a wider context. It has been exhilarating and exhausting, inspiring and illuminating. It is an occasion for renewed gratitude for those who have supported me through the years and at the moments when I needed them most. It has also highlighted what matters most to me – my connections, my faith, my friends, and my family.

BELONGING

Since I was a teenager, I have felt a deep need to belong to something larger than myself, to focus my time and energy on service and giving back as part of an organization that can make an impact in people's lives. I have joined several major groups, typically composed of African-American women, to fulfill this desire with meaningful action, and Chenits and the children have participated in similar organizations. These commitments helped us stay connected to our heritage even when we lived in neighborhoods with few African-Americans.

When I was in high school, my grandmother encouraged me to join Eastern Star. We marched in parades and held fundraising events such as bobbing for apples that united young people to serve others. I eagerly enlisted my friends: "Margaret will sign you up for all kinds of things," they said.

In college, a friend of mine and I joined Angel Flight, the first African-Americans in the group that performed significant community service for the community in Pittsburgh near campus. I had seen how it helped our neighbors. I also joined the Some of God's Children Chorus, a singing group that sought to uplift others.

As a mother of young children, I did the typical mom fundraisers such as selling candy in the neighborhood to raise money for good causes. I joined Jack and Jill of America to volunteer and to make sure my children would learn about life through opportunities not otherwise available. Jack and Jill has some elitist elements, but it has benefited my children and grandchildren as they navigate the double consciousness required of African-Americans.

I pledged the Alpha Kappa Alpha Sorority, a historic African-American institution (Senator Kamala Harris is a member) focused on service to humanity while helping members build social capital, including mentors and sponsors who accelerate their careers.

I am an active member volunteering in many service projects. Chenits belongs to Alpha Phi Alpha Fraternity, the first African-American Greek organization when it was organized at Howard University. The group established the monument in Washington honoring its member Rev. Martin Luther King Jr.

I also belong to Northeasterners, an organization of married African-American women founded in the northeastern United States during the Roaring Twenties for social interaction. More recently I joined The Links, an organization for African-American women, despite its elitist qualities – I hope to find rewarding outlets for service. Money and time prevent such involvement for many people, and I guard my values of inclusion, empathy, and commitment to service not always valued in the group. Chenits belongs to Boulé of Sigma Pi Phi Fraternity, which has some of the same elitism but seems to uphold its principles of service. These commitments, which require significant contributions, require a delicate balance with our religious commitments.

Active membership in these affiliations is for life, and we work hard to fulfill our responsibilities. They are often generational – our children, then our grandchildren, belonged to Jack and Jill, and some of our children are Alphas. They have been significant in the lives of many African-Americans, often helping them move forward professionally. For me, they also address the need to belong – not only to make friends, which happens naturally with like-minded people, but to have a vehicle for impactful service.

FAITH AND FEAR

My ability to grow beyond the limits of my past, beyond the limits others put on my color and gender, beyond the limits of my own hopes and dreams, is grounded in the confidence that I am not doing this alone – someone bigger (often called God) is with me and making the progress possible. My personal faith, forged in the nitty-gritty of my life experiences and sometimes in contrast to the norms of conventional religion, has provided empowerment and purpose for becoming the best version of myself as I seek to find contentment in knowing that God is content with me.

My first experience of faith came at Mount Rose Baptist Church in Uniontown, the core of my childhood with my family and friends. There I was baptized before I was a teenager. There I was taught to surround myself with like-minded people who believed the truths the church taught. I learned to seek my purpose in the context of acknowledging the One in charge of my life. Those elements have remained through life – the power in knowing that someone is looking after me beyond the fallible people with that role, the constant search for a better me, the awareness that being content with my life means knowing God is content with what can give. Even as a child, I felt free to speak my mind, choose my direction, and become all I could become.

My teen years challenged that faith. The judgment and condescension from people because of the color of my skin eroded my confidence. My out-of-wedlock pregnancy scandalized by relatives and fellow churchgoers and wounded relationships with people who had cared about me. Many labeled me an unforgivable sinner. I had to rethink my relationship with God as I dealt with disappointment, anger, and lack of trust – this time from people who look like me. Shaken by this treatment, I considered finding another congregation or another religion, maybe Islam or Jehovah's Witnesses, or even no God at all. This brand of Christianity was not what I needed to become the person I wanted to be as I struggled to create a life for myself and my son.

While I was trying to find my way back to a personal relationship with God, I was singing in a college gospel chorus called Some of God's Children that performed on campus and at nearby universities. Once we sang at a Pentecostal church – we called them Holy Rollers – and the preacher issued an invitation to reconnect, recommit, and find a new path to what God wanted us to be. That sounded like me, so I went forward and joined the line of people waiting to be touched and prayed with by the elders and ministers. My emotions surged, and I wept – I was trying to find how I could live right for myself, my family, and others. As the minister put his hand on my head to pray, I felt him push me away. People behind grabbed me and shook me so others thought I was having a powerful supernatural experience. But I wasn't shaking. I was a prop for their show. When they finished, I walked to my seat and sat quietly. This only exacerbated my doubts. I was trying to navigate my life as one of two African-American students in a toxic nursing program, I was trying to help this church raise money for its mission, and I felt used. Nevertheless, I knew many people who had overcome the challenges of life on the strength of faith, and I was still seeking that power.

I was convinced that I was here for a purpose, and I needed to find it. I had to work hard to discover who I really was – my values, my ethics, my place in this world. That involved my blackness. Could I accept all of me, all the positives and negatives of being in this skin? Could I be a role model and a light for others like me who wake up every single morning facing the fact of being black in America? For a time, I was less than my best – using profanity that shocked even me, expressing anger, being biased toward others. Those traits damage the person more than the others.

How did I get here? Not "How did African-Americans get in this position?" but "How did I as an individual wind up in this space?" I had to understand myself before I could see the bigger picture. I had earned my role as a nurse, but my skills were questioned based on the color of my skin. My bachelor's and advanced degrees were no protection against discrimination because my employer, my patients, and even my professional peers perceived me as less-than. Patients didn't want my care; employers scheduled unfair hours. I identified with Job – even as a child, I had questioned where a kind and forgiving God was when he endured all that suffering. How could a good God put African-Americans through what we have suffered for centuries, for over 400 years?

As I began to travel more for work, I realized that all over the world, people with darker skin were always treated as less-than. On my first trip to the slave castles of Ghana, I wept at how noble people had been deceived into giving up their own children and villages for profit. I saw the beautiful Catholic churches, declaring the glory of God, built above the slave caves. All these enslaved people, even the ones who didn't survive the crossing, believed God's will was done. I thought about my ancestors' experience in this country down to me – the ancestors who didn't look like me as well as the ones who were shackled and starved. I vowed to make this world a better place by helping people over-come anger and disappointment and all the things I was trying to figure out for myself through faith.

I wanted to continue the fight even though I was not accepted abroad even by people who looked like me, people who considered their legacy greater than mine. I could be the most educated professional in the room, but others would look to the white man, the white woman, the white student ahead of me because of my color – until a white person gave permission to address their questions to Dr. Pettigrew. Many of those situ-ations involved people who were conducting medical missions in the name of God, but they rarely met Afri-can-Americans because our people were preoccupied with seeking justice at home. While I was performing surgery and taking care of patients, most of the team would be out spreading the word of the Lord.

Even at home, I was alone in raising my children in the Christianity I had known – Chenits was not part of that. I wanted to send them to Sunday school, to be with them in church, to teach them of the undeserved gift of grace that made them good inside. But even as an adult, I struggled with what faith and grace and God's purpose really meant for me.

The answer came largely in my encounters with patients. As a doctor, I saw people as they really are, with the masks off – the raw fear and anguish that come both from a devastating medical diagnosis and from the daily social, economic, personal struggles they shared – how to feed my family, how to live with a cheating husband, how to raise my children while hiding my HIV diagnosis. An old white man bared his soul to me, apologized for his bias, wished me well. A woman with a fatal disease let me hold her white hand in my black one when there was nothing else I could do. Through them, I began to understand that I can be all of me, a better me, if I could really understand what faith and grace meant for the total me.

That's where I'm living today. It redefines joy. It upholds me through the challenges of confronting bias. I still seek the place where I am content – rather, where I know God is content with me. I can find peace like never before. I can find the faith to climb out of the pit where I find myself each day. I still question whether I have done all I can; as I tell students: "When you think you can't do more, you can do more." But the strength to do that comes from grace and faith.

That faith finds expression in three different ways, three different places of worship in my life. The first is when I am alone – what Christians call the "prayer closet" – where I can really hear the peace and calm of my God. I can close my eyes and know that no matter what, God is going to be proud of my life because God is working with me. The second is when I am united with other people – friends, family, or anyone who welcomes me to be uplifted, reassured, empowered; where I can tell them how good they are, how important they are, without boundaries like race or age. I get there often.

The third is a traditional house of worship. It has not been easy to find such a place in black American culture when I have a gay son and many family members who don't look like me. I have walked away from congregations who say HIV is God's punishment for sin. I understand why some people never find a home in organized religion, but both Chenits and I are grateful for Macedonia Baptist Church in Pittsburgh's Hill District. We started visiting soon after we returned to Pittsburgh in 2002 and joined in 2004. Even when we are out of the country, we listen to the streaming service of our young minister whose message empowers, illumines, and comforts me.

But is this enough to erase the fear I have carried for myself and my loved ones my entire life? To be honest: No. I fear for my family and others who look like me because our black or brown faces confront a society that judges first by color. I am frightened when, despite reality, I am judged by structural and reflexive bias and racism. For example, I recently had a minor fender bender in a hospital parking lot. I hit a parked car. I pulled over, called the police and placed a note on the car for the owner to contact me for repairs. I waited for the police, who arrived promptly – a short, stocky white police officer who was friendly and very professional. As I phoned in the event to my insurance company, he called in my license plate to the dispatcher. I am not sure if this happens with all fender/benders but assumed it was protocol. After a few minutes on the phone, he told me in a very stern voice to hang up the phone. I hung up the phone and was told not to move from my position, there was a problem with my plates. He asked several questions about my vehicle, ownership and other prying questions about my possible infractions. I have none. I reassured him that I was the owner and there must be some mistake. I asked him to call it in again as it was obvious that he was becoming annoyed and did not believe me. He called in the plates again. I listened as the dispatcher told him that the plates belonged to a gray pickup with the same Ohio plates that had been stolen. "Ohio." I drive a black Toyota with 180,000 miles on it with Pennsylvania license plates. I told the officer this fact. They ran the plates again and they matched. He relaxed, but I didn't as he began to discuss our mutual military service and the commitment to die for our country. I am not sure when I feared for my safety, but I am sure a medical evaluation would have resulted in a noted elevation of blood pressure, pulse, and catecholamines that indicated preparations to fight or take flight. What made this officer believe that I was potential criminal? Standing in the parking lot, calling the police, placing a note on the damaged care and wearing a beautiful suit with a hospital badge didn't prevent him from seeing the color of my skin. No matter how many degrees, level of education or financial stature protects anyone who looks like me from being judged and potentially placed in danger from a group of folks that are sworn to protect and serve. If anyone doubts that the movement of Black Live Matter is essential to save black lives, they are living with their heads stuck in the sand or they just don't care. This is only one example of the toxic macro- and micro-aggressions that people of color face daily. Fear is real. Faith is necessary to survive the many fear-inducing events we as people of color regularly experience. Some claim that fear and faith cannot exist together. Not in my world.

WHAT'S IN A NAME?

MARGARET

Margaret, my name, has not always been a proud source of comfort. When I was a child, I never knew anyone with that name who looked like me. Growing up I preferred to use my middle name Dela, short for Delarese. Della Reese was a black beautiful female artist with a tremendous following from both black and white races. I have come to understand that the name has rich meaning. I imagine it as the name of my great-great-grandmother because I believe she was a strong and proud African woman who became the bed warmer of Sidney Lee in hopes of a better life and legacy for her offspring.

Two other Margaret's came into my life who made me the woman I am today, living black, proud, and hopeful that my children and grandchildren will become their greatest selves, will be seen, heard, respected, and appreciated for who they are.

MARGARET WILLIAMS

Margaret Williams looked like the glamorous women on television that many young girls, including me, dreamed of becoming in the 1950s and early 1960s: five-feet-seven, petite, blond, married to the man she loved, and white. But her real life was the opposite of those pampered, bejeweled princesses in the shows, because the man she loved was black. That was unheard-of in polite society, and her marriage to Slick Williams was illegal in more than half the states. Her family disowned her; her friends abandoned her. They twisted the lovers into evidence for the myth of the oversexed black male. Many of the African-Americans among whom she lived mistrusted her – her skin was the color of the oppressor, and women feared she provided an example for black men who might be tempted by women outside of their race. Somehow they overlooked the fact that none of us is pure – the mark of white slave owners in our bloodlines is visible in our various shades.

The couple were my parents' best friends, and Margaret, my namesake, was godmother to me and my sister Faith – a loving couple appointed to adopt us if anything happened to Momma and Daddy. The two couples' affection and conversation yielded abundant life lessons. Slick worked with Daddy in the coal mines just over the line in Fairmont, West Virginia, and Margaret kept house on a beautiful home place in Uniontown, where I helped her tend the garden and vineyard in the summertime. She nurtured us, disciplining with a gentle touch and a lesson on forgiveness no matter what we did. One summer, we were squeezing grapes together and attracted a swarm of bees; I got stung more times than I could count. Margaret put me in a cool bath and held me until I stopped crying.

We didn't go back to Uniontown often after we moved to McKeesport when I was eight, but whenever Daddy drove us there in his big Oldsmobile, we would stop to see Margaret and Slick. Slick died young, and Margaret never remarried. She moved into a one-bedroom house behind Mount Rose Baptist Church, which we had attended together, and stayed active on the missionary and usher boards, in the choir, and at service projects. She was always eager to talk about her church work. She never worked outside her home; now she depended on Slick's pension and local handouts to sustain her and her many pampered cats. I saw her often enough to watch her age gracefully and never regret her choices. Margaret was proud of my accomplishments – she attended my high school and college graduations, and she knew the odds I had overcome.

"You are not finished with such important work," she told me. "You are an asset to your family, your race, your community, and the world. Know that the role of 'first' may never end for you." Later in life, I realized that the woman who spoke those words loved me unconditionally, understood the breadth and depth of racism, yet believed that I would overcome. When she died, Momma, Faith, and I cleaned the lifetime of memories from the little home where she had lived happily as a white among the coloreds.

Margaret means "Pearl," and I liked to think my mother gave me that name because she saw me as a precious gem like her friend. I needed validation and self-worth wherever I could get it. Margaret and Slick had no children of their own, but her maternal love for me shaped my view of race – in my worst moments of anger at white people in later years, she remained the counter-example that helped me rise above color. She taught me that I could love and be loved regardless of color. She reassured me that hate, abuse, and lack of dignity and respect for "coloreds," as we were known, was a strategy to maintain white wealth and privilege that would erode over time. She convinced me that most white folks are good people misguided by a false doctrine of white supremacy. Through all the challenges and dark times of the rest of my life, she remained in memory as a teacher and a healer.

MARGARET CARVER

A few years ago, when I came across my birth certificate, Chenits pointed out that the physician who delivered me was named Margaret. I researched her and was astonished to discover the many ways our lives had run in parallel since the day Dr. Margaret Carver guided me out of my mother's womb and into the world. She had died a few years earlier, in 2013, at age 92. This white woman's story has become a treasured part of my own personal and professional understanding although we never knew one another.

Margaret earned her undergraduate dual degree in biology and chemistry from Margaret Morrison College at Carnegie Mellon in 1943. After working as a chemist through World War II, she enrolled in the University of Pittsburgh School of Medicine in 1946 and was one of seven women who graduated in 1950, along with eighty men. After her internship in Harrisburg, she settled in Uniontown to practice in 1952, two years before she delivered me. She was the first female doctor in this small town in over twenty years. Margaret became a board-certified obstetrician/gynecologist in 1961 after studying at Millard Fillmore Hospital in Buffalo, New York. She then went on to deliver another ten thousand babies in her forty-five-year career in Uniontown. She was chief of obstetrics and gynecology at Uniontown Hospital for thirty years and led the opening of the first mental health and family planning clinics.

"I enjoy practicing obstetrics and gynecology. It is a happy specialty," Margaret said in an interview after she retired. "Everybody's joyful when you bring a baby into the world. They are beautiful little creatures."

I feel a deep kinship with this stranger. I imagine she gave up a promising career as a clinical scientist to care for the people in Uniontown, including my parents, who needed her. I expect my delivery was in a segregated maternity ward, in the days before family members were present to support the mother and pain medication was rarely offered to African-Americans. The staff was likely unkind to a poor black twenty-year-old woman with an eighth-grade education who was having her third baby. It's not hard to imagine the remarks – I still hear them today.

I imagine Margaret at the foot of my mother's bed, telling her as I have with countless women: "Take a deep breath. Push. I'm going to count up to ten. You give me all you've got. You're having your baby. Only you can do this. This is between you and your baby."

This young white woman who dedicated her life to this profession was blessing me with her hands. Did she imagine that this little black baby would grow up to be a doctor? I imagine her catching my body and telling my mom: "Here's your little girl. She's precious. Ten fingers and ten toes."

I want to believe she was kind and gentle and loving and saw the miracle in what she'd done because she'd done it so many times before, she never got tired of feeling its part of God's plan, as I feel every time I help my patients. I want to believe she knew she was giving my mom a gift, she was giving the world a gift, and she was very, very happy to be part of my birth – and part of the life I have lived. This was the beginning of my journey to see clearly the colors of my heart. What's in a name? A life story.

GROWING OLD TOGETHER

For forty-six years and counting, Chenits has kept his promise. I had nearly lost him to a cerebral hemorrhage in Jacksonville, Florida, in October 2000. Chenits was working at Florida Community College; I remained on active duty serving in the Navy. One night after a long day, Chenits and I turned in early to catch up on some needed rest. I awakened to find Chenits had left our bed and was making moaning sounds in the bathroom. I called out to him asking him if he was ok. He replied by telling me that he had the worst headache in his life. I found him with his hands raised holding his head. These were signs that he was having a stroke, a possible cranial hemorrhage. He was unconscious by the time he reached the hospital. After three days in the ICU, he awakened. The bleeding had stopped. Chenits returned to the work he loved after six months of rest and rehabilitation. Our focus turned to health and wellbeing. Together, we joined Weight Watchers, took long walks, and made exercise a priority.

One brush with death wasn't enough to test our clear understanding that only "Grace" enables us to continue to work together and grow together as a couple. We nearly lost that opportunity when Chenits suffered a heart attack in 2015.

It was an early Saturday morning, February 14, Valentine's Day. It was a cold, snowy day as we slept late before discussing what our celebration would look like. Our traditional Valentine's Day celebration consisted of a trip to the Tavern in New Wilmington, Pennsylvania. The Tavern is an old Victorian home built in 1849. It stands as family landmark, a renovated home now a restaurant that was part of the Underground Railroad, freeing blacks who fled from the South.

Chenits and I continue to celebrate our togetherness at the Tavern on special occasions. As we made plans that day, which included a drive to the Tavern, Chenits commented on his long work week and the fatigue he felt walking to and from his office. He said he had started to have a little chest pain during the night but it had worsened during our conversation. I questioned him as any physician would to explore whether he may be experiencing the signs of a heart attack. His symptoms were atypical. He complained of mid-chest pain, non-radiating without arm or jaw pain. None of the typical warning signs. He became restless and felt the need to start the day with making breakfast for me. As he began to leave our bedroom, he turned, looked at me, and said the pain was unbearable. I insisted that he return to bed as I called 911. As I was speaking to the operator, Chenits got out of bed, now confused and disoriented. I managed to break his fall and place him on the floor as he began to have a grand mal seizure. He was no longer conscious, unable to hear my pleas to stay with me. He couldn't see the panic on my face as I dropped my physician mode for the identity of a wife who loved this kind and gentle man. My soulmate was slipping away.

My grief overwhelmed the operator as she shouted for me to leave him for a moment, open the door and let help in. After the placement of stents and a short stay in the intensive care unit, Chenits was discharged to cardiac rehab, back in my arms and ready to continue his passion and purpose of caring for others, beginning with me. People ask how we've managed to stay together for so many years and still support one another. It's about the journey we are taking together – the decision, no matter what, to move forward, never forgetting but being able to forgive, saying I'm sorry, saying I love you, being in love. At one point in Chenits' life, he decided he was finished with religion. – "I paid my dues," he said. I struggled with a marriage that lacked shared faith and practice, but I knew I could safely stay with him. I watched God bring him back to the faith, trust and relationship with God that has functioned to make us both stronger. Many scars don't go away. They are a constant reminder and proof that wounds *do* heal.

EPILOGUE

Somehow "something blue" became the motif of our fortieth-anniversary vows renewal in the Albertson Wedding Chapel on La Brea Avenue in Los Angeles in October 2018 – my shoes, Chenits' cummerbund and tie. But as I looked across the palette of faces in the chairs of bright silver and white, I saw the colors of my heart – the spectrum of African-Americans from deep ebony to near-passable pale; the Caucasian white of in-laws; the beautifully-blended babies that some of those unions had produced. The shades of their skin, the textures of their hair, long sources of individual identity and often-fraught engagement with the larger society and within their communities, all belonged together here because they belonged with us. This was our life.

It was the fourth renewal of our vows, and Chenits and I had chosen the chapel in Los Angeles where we wed for this fresh start with our three sons, Carlos, Chenits Reese, and Gaetan; my brother Herb; and a few close friends from those early days when we set out for California from Pittsburgh, far from our origins, to establish our family in our own way. Rather than marking traditional quarter-centuries, we renew whenever we want to remember our commitment to enrich each person's life, our lives together, and our world.

Our small wedding in 1978 had sealed my Cinderella dream that a hero on a white horse would sweep me up and take care of me for life – never mind that our reality, as for most African-American families from before slavery days, meant my working outside the home and long seasons of separation. Our happily-ever-after was to be together.

At twenty years, we reaffirmed with our whole family at a friend's house in Jacksonville, Florida, after Chenits's stroke. Five years later, our children organized a major celebration with a host of friends and family celebrating twenty-five years of marriage.

At thirty years, we were in Swaziland in South Africa, a patriarchal, polygamous society where I had been working as a medical professional with women to combat the highest incidence of HIV/AIDS in the world. We chose to renew in the African motherland, so central to our life and work, with ceremonies connected to our ancient legacy – Chenits wore a loincloth, I wore sheep's wool, women surrounded me after we were separated for ritual prayers.

The fortieth renewal, at the root of our union, was a celebration of family. Chenits and I wrote the ceremony. Gaetan officiated. Chenits Reese recited a poem of our move to California and our life as a family. Carlos read Psalm 139 about God's intimate knowledge of us, which reflects our life and purpose even before we knew ourselves. Herb welcomed me down the aisle and sang Bobby Caldwell's "What You Won't Do for Love."

"Chenits, you are my lover, my friend, my confidant, my teacher," I told him. "I am so blessed that God chose you to place in my life. I am so grateful that you chose me. I love you."

"For me, you have been written into my destiny from the beginning," Chenits told me. "I was on the path to a love that has only grown stronger. Through the transition of our life together, you have been lover, partner, and friend."

Our reception was held at the home of Herb and Mick, my sister-in-law, where a DJ played. After everyone else left, Chenits and I stayed in California for five days to reflect on our life, our love, and how each of us — individually and together — has flourished and found ways to navigate the realities of being African-Americans, of bringing up African-American sons, in a world that is changing and an America that still has much changing to do.

This is my story of living in that society as a daughter, sister, schoolgirl, girlfriend, wife, mother, nurse, soldier, physician, aunt, great-aunt, grandmother, great-grandmother, and advocate for women's health around the world. It stretches from the DNA evidence of my ancient legacy in Africa and elsewhere, across the backdrop of my ancestors' experience of slavery, segregation, Great Depression, and war, and through my firsthand encounters with poverty, discrimination, affirmative action, police violence, HIV/AIDS, and same-sex marriage. I tell my story through tears and laughter, anger and disappointment, fear, and love.

The most satisfying fruit of my life is the palette that greeted me in the Albertson Chapel — my family of origin, the family that Chenits and I have produced, the friends and in-laws that have become a part of us across the decades — the colors of my heart. My hope is that unity in difference, that *E pluribus unum*, that dignified personhood, solidarity, and celebration of common good, will become a reality for our nation and our world. This unity continues to unfold for us.

NOTABLE BOOK COMMENTS

Dr. Margaret Larkins-Pettigrew's story is an inspiring account of how the twists and turns of life for a woman of color inevitably include the realities of racism and sexism, on one hand, and the difference family and faith can make on the other hand. Colors of My Heart reveals some difficult truths of a doctor who has devoted her life to making a difference, not only in her family and her community, but for the human family in the United States and around the world. The good doctor is to be congratulated for telling some difficult truths of African American life in her own family and in this nation, but she clearly comes through it all with a heart full of love and with a commitment to equity and social justice for this generation and the next.

~ MARILYN SANDERS MOBLEY, PHD
PROFESSOR OF ENGLISH AND AFRICAN AMERICAN STUDIES
FORMER VICE PRESIDENT FOR INCLUSION, DIVERSITY AND
EQUAL OPPORTUNITY
CASE WESTERN RESERVE

Wow! I couldn't stop reading. Dr. Margaret Larkins-Pettigrew's life story took me on an insightful and thought-provoking journey. Her discovery of self as a black woman living in America exposes the double consciousness, micro and macro- aggressions and internal racial conflicts that challenges many minoritized individuals' experience as they pursue their passion with purpose. She has done this and more rising above fear with the support of faith and family.

~ DANIEL SIMON, MD
PRESIDENT, UNIVERSITY HOSPITAL CLEVELAND MEDICAL
CENTER

Made in the USA
Las Vegas, NV
28 November 2020